lonely planet

ANDY ROUSE

WILDLIFE
TRAVEL PHOTOGRAPHY

A GUIDE TO TAKING BETTER PICTURES

LONELY PLANET OFFICES

AUSTRALIA
Head Office
Locked Bag 1, Footscray, Victoria 3011
☎ 03 8379 8000, fax 03 8379 8111
talk2us@lonelyplanet.com.au

UK
72–82 Rosebery Ave,
Clerkenwell, London EC1R 4RW
☎ 020 7841 9000, fax 020 7841 9001
go@lonelyplanet.co.uk

USA
150 Linden St, Oakland, CA 94607
☎ 510 893 8555, toll free 800 275 8555
fax 510 893 8572, info@lonelyplanet.com

Wildlife Photography: A Guide to Taking Better Pictures
1st edition June 2006
ISBN 1 74059 900 4

Published by Lonely Planet Publications Pty Ltd
ABN 36 005 607 983

text © Lonely Planet 2006
photographs © Andy Rouse 2006

Cover photograph: Grizzly bear, Alaska, USA

CONTENTS

THE AUTHOR

Andy Rouse has built a worldwide reputation as one of the very best professional wildlife photographers. Having now fully embraced the digital era, he has spent over a decade travelling to all corners of the globe in search of the cuddly and the cute, as well as the dark and the dangerous. Andy initially established his name with unique images that others were reluctant to try for, and his fearlessness earned him awards of the highest level, including BBC Wildlife Photographer of the Year.

Since then, his enormous collection of images – along with those of his partner, Tracey Rich, a fellow pro-photographer, author and zoologist – has burgeoned into one of the best wildlife photography stock libraries currently online. Andy's interest in digital technology has also led him to become a specialist in the RAW format of digital photography (a noncompressed form of digital image) and he is in constant demand for his expertise.

Veteran creator of more than 10 books, plus two television series that detail his work and have been shown throughout the world, Andy's presentation style endears him to a wide audience. He enjoys sharing his knowledge and experience with others and can often be found running courses, leading international expeditions and giving highly entertaining talks both at home in the UK and abroad.

From the Author

Having the ability to travel around the globe as a professional wildlife photographer is a privilege I have never underestimated or taken for granted. Having spent many hundreds of days and many thousands of hours learning by trial and error how to achieve those award-winning shots, I am really pleased to be able to impart some of the hints and tips, skills and techniques I have gained from all that time spent in the field. Travel is a superb means by which to see and experience some of the greatest natural wonders of the world. I hope that the guidance of this book will enable you to capture these images with your camera with minimal effort and with far fewer instances of a numb backside than it has taken me.

Wildlife photography is something that comes from the heart, not the head, but knowing the basics of how to get the most from your wildlife encounters will greatly enhance your experience. It will also allow you to capture those unique memories and to share them with others for years to come. After all, that's what photography is all about – having fun, so enjoy!

THIS BOOK

From the Publisher

This book was produced in Lonely Planet's Melbourne office. It was commissioned by Bridget Blair and series editor Richard I'Anson. Jenny Bilos managed the project with assistance from Jo Vraca. The book was edited by Adrienne Costanzo and Laura Gibb, designed by Brendan Dempsey and laid out by Kaitlin Beckett and Jacqui Saunders. Mark Adams designed the cover artwork and Ryan Evans managed pre-press preparation of the photographs.

Using this Book

You may be wondering if this book will be another wildlife book full of technical jargon, packed with images taken with fantastically overpriced equipment. Well, fear not. This book reflects the sort of equipment that most keen amateurs have – affordable, flexible and light. Captions have been deliberately written to appeal to travelling wildlife photographers – people who want to maximise the wonderful opportunities travelling the world can give in terms of experiencing wildlife; people who wish to have images that they can be proud of and that do their experiences justice. Flexibility is the theme throughout this book, which emphasises the use of minimal equipment to cover the widest range of potential opportunities you might experience. Remember: possessing a long lens and a head full of technical mumbo jumbo does not make you a great wildlife photographer – the essence is an appreciation of your subject. Above all you must really love animals. That includes everything that walks, crawls or flies – you need to appreciate it in all its glory. Wildlife photography should be seen as an excuse to spend time with animals in their own habitats, absorbing the way they live. But above all it is all about having fun; don't forget it!

The Author's Approach

Wildlife photography for me is not a career or a job – it is a passion and a way of life. It is something I have to do on a regular basis or I become very grumpy indeed. From my perspective there is no better experience than working hard to get close to an animal in its natural environment and being rewarded with a few precious moments in its company. A great picture is a bonus, not a necessity.

My approach to capturing that perfect shot has always been a little different from most. In the early days of my career most commentators thought that I had a death wish, as I had a tendency to get suicidally close to large mammals such as polar bears, elephants and hippos. In truth, I had no desire to kill myself – I just loved getting close to animals. Now, I still get close to animals because that is the essence of my work, but I take a far more considered approach to the wildlife I encounter and getting as close as possible is not necessary under most circumstances.

When I am planning a trip, thorough research will indicate the kind of equipment I will need to take. If I'm working with very shy animals then I'll need a different set of equipment from that required on an expedition cruise. I adjust my kit bag accordingly, but generally it will contain a mix of the following items:

▶ Canon EOS 1Ds MKI and MKII bodies
▶ 500mm f4L lens (used on about 50% of my trips)
▶ 300mm f2.8L lens
▶ 100-400mm or 70-200mm f2.8L lens
▶ 20mm lens
▶ 1.4x teleconverter and extension tube
▶ 4 x 4 GB and 4 x 2 GB Integral I-Pro CF (compact flash) memory cards
▶ Jobo GigaVu portable downloader
▶ Pentax Optio compact digital
▶ Gitzo 1548 tripod with either a Kirk Ballhead with Wimberley Sidekick or a conventional Wimberley tripod head
▶ Various accessories, such as a tool kit, cable release and cleaning kit
▶ Lee Filters circular polariser and holder
▶ Empty beanbags, clamps
▶ Electrical kit (chargers and spare cables)
▶ Binoculars (usually 10 x 42, which are light but of superb optical quality for low-light work)
▶ Outdoor clothing (eg Páramo)
▶ Rucksacks to carry it all in (eg Crumpler and Lowepro)

Now, you will notice that I do have some expensive kit. I have to, because this is my livelihood, but it is not essential for keen amateurs. My images have to be of the utmost quality, even in the lowest levels of light, because the standard of professional wildlife photography is so high. The fundamental thing for me is to take the absolute minimum when travelling, not only to reduce potential hassles with transportation and security but also to save my poor back!

Photo Captions

The photo captions in this book have been provided to demonstrate technique and equipment. Apart from describing the wildlife shown, the captions give the most relevant technical details:

▶ Camera model and lens
▶ Exposure (aperture and shutter speed, ISO)
▶ Accessories used (flash, tripods etc)

Giant otter, the Pantanal, Brazil

Wildlife photography is a way of life for me and nothing makes it more special than when I get a chance to photograph an animal that approaches me of its own free will. This image of a giant otter shows one such time. A relaxed and happy animal always makes for a better photograph, because the shot is taken on its terms and not those of the person behind the lens.

◀ 35mm SLR, 500mm F4L lens, 1/250 f5.6, Provia 400F, tripod

INTRODUCTION

Wildlife photography is one of the most challenging photographic genres and requires a mixture and mastery of skills from areas such as sports photography, landscape and social photography and portraiture, as well as a small element of the voyeuristic paparazzi.

The two biggest challenges to the wildlife photographer are:

▶ Finding your subject in the first place. Most subjects do not go out of their way to be photographed – you have to work at getting the shot. Of course there are exceptions, such as penguins, who are everyone's best friend, but such cases are rare.

▶ When you do find your subject, the encounter is often relatively short, so you have to work very quickly and efficiently. The photographer who fiddles around with the camera, position, lighting and anything else rather than simply taking the shot will not be very successful at any level of wildlife photography. Throughout this book you will see a simple approach to photography which allows you to shoot very quickly and effectively. This is the one reason that professionals consistently get superb-quality shots. With this collection of very simple pointers you can do the same, too. It is not rocket science.

Light is essential to a great wildlife image, but to be fair this is largely beyond your control, because it is dictated by the subject's activity period and the light the subject is in when you manage to find it. Sometimes you simply have to make the best of the situation.

Gull, west coast, Norway

A wildlife encounter may last for several hours but it is more likely to be over in a matter of seconds. To get great wildlife shots you need to be ready for anything – at a moment's notice.

◀ 35mm DSLR, 300mm f2.8L lens, 1/1000 f4, ISO 100 RAW

African Lion, Masai Mara National Reserve, Kenya
◀ DSLR, 500mm lens, 1/125 f4, ISO 100 RAW, beanbag

PART ONE

THE GEAR

Great wildlife photography comes from the heart and not the head, but one great step in achieving that great image is having the right gear for the purpose. This doesn't mean you have to have the most expensive or the latest equipment to take good wildlife photographs, but you must have a thorough knowledge of the right kit for the right situation and how to use it properly. Camera equipment is merely a tool used to achieve the images you desire, and here we will discover the basic kit you'll need to cover every eventuality. The trouble with photographing wildlife is that you never quite know what's going to happen next, but that's what makes it so exciting, too.

Siberian tiger drinking, Dartmoor Wildlife Park, England
◀ 35mm SLR, 80-200mm lens, 1/60 f5.6, Fujichrome 100

EQUIPMENT

To be able to shoot quickly and effectively and make the most of any wildlife you may encounter, you will need only the minimum of equipment, as having too much choice can often lead to missed shots. If you have a bag full of lenses then you'll either be trying to constantly change them or be thinking about changing them. Either way you'll become distracted and that memorable shot is likely to be missed. For the majority of photographers, getting all your kit into a single, manageable photographic rucksack is your prime consideration. If you can achieve this, you will be rewarded by greater flexibility and a hassle-free trip, and you'll also avoid back problems and orang-utan arms.

And finally, familiarity with your equipment will pay dividends when you are travelling. If you refer to the camera manual when a leopard is posing for you on a termite mound, you will not only lose a memorable shot but you will regret it forever.

CAMERAS

You will not get far in your travelling wildlife photography without one, so the choice of camera in relation to your level of interest, cost and skill is an important choice. Wildlife photography is one of the most difficult photographic genres but yields some of the greatest rewards in terms of once-in-a-lifetime experiences. Capturing that all-important moment is a tall order, but one that you should strive to achieve to the best of your ability. Knowing the advantages and limitations of your equipment, whether it's a compact or an SLR (single-lens reflex), digital or film, is essential to getting it right and returning home with an image of that moment that you can share with others.

Single-Lens Reflex Cameras – Digital & Film

An SLR, film or digital, is the ideal camera for capturing wildlife images because it allows you the greatest flexibility. It will allow you numerous options to change film speed, shutter speed and all manner of shooting parameters, enabling you to capture or create the image that you want – your own original take on the subject. Likewise, the SLR has the greatest range of lenses available to allow you to photograph anything from an ant's knees to a giraffe's eyeball – all with the same camera, regardless of whether it is film or digital.

Any discussion about cameras these days will naturally centre on the digital SLR (DSLR). The film camera has been developed about as far as it can go and the majority of cameras sold today are of the digital era. Film cameras still abound but are becoming increasingly surpassed by their digital descendants and most people will at some time have to confront the issue of going digital and choosing from the myriad digital cameras available.

It is likely that your decision as to which DSLR to buy will be based on price and the existing lenses you possess rather than which sensor it uses or the extent to which it possesses all the latest bells and whistles. (For a full explanation of the technical aspects of a DSLR, look in Lonely Planet's *Travel Photography: A Guide to Taking Better Pictures* or the *DSLR Handbook*; see p170.) Although there is a lot to learn about a DSLR, there is essentially very little that you need to know to be able to use one effectively; it is very easy to use and a fantastic tool for the travelling wildlife photographer. The following are a few points to consider when choosing a DSLR.

Quality

DSLR quality is expressed in megapixels (MP), which is basically the number of pixels within the camera's digital sensor. The bottom line is that any DSLR quoted to have

Scarlet macaw, Honduras
◀ 35mm SLR, 70-200mm lens, 1/200 f8, Velvia 50

Verreaux' sifaka dancing, Réserve Privée de Berenty (Berenty Reserve), Madagascar

To be honest, very little separates one film camera from another, apart from motor-drive speed and the legendary Nikon matrix metering system. This image benefited from the 6fps (frames per second) motor drive, but it could have been taken with any make of film camera with a similar drive speed, as experience more than makes up for any differences between manufacturers' metering systems.

◀ 35mm SLR, 70-200mm lens, 1/500 f4, Provia 100F

8 MP (eight million pixels) or greater will produce great A3 prints and will be more than a match for a scanned high-quality (such as Fuji Velvia) film image. Unless you are a budding professional, there is really no need to buy a top-of-the-range DSLR. It is much better to go for a good-quality 8 MP camera and put the money you save towards new lenses, other equipment or a place on a photographic course or expedition dedicated to wildlife photography.

Buffer Size

The one negative aspect of using DSLRs is that they all have a finite number of images they can store in their internal memory before they need to write them to the memory card. This number is called the buffer size; when it is reached, the DSLR will effectively prevent you from taking any more shots while your images are written safely to the card. As wildlife photographers, this is especially annoying, as animals tend to move a lot. Buffer lockout, as it is called, should be thought of as running out of and changing film. It can be simply managed by being selective about the pictures you take rather than keeping your finger on the motor-drive button. This will ensure that your camera will not be busy writing to the drive at a crucial moment, preventing you from taking any more shots. Buffer size is not something that can be determined by you, apart from shooting JPEG instead of RAW (see p16).

ANDY ROUSE/GETTY IMAGES

Gentoo penguin surfing, Sea Lion Island, Falkland Islands

Modern DSLRs are used for high-action photography all over the world – you just have to learn to work with the buffer limitations of the system you own. This fun image was taken with a DSLR specially designed for action, with an 8fps drive and fast autofocus to match. Even so, when taking the shot the trick is not to blast away but to pick exactly what you want and only take that. This method will ensure that even if you have the smallest buffer you will hardly ever get locked out.

▲ DSLR, 300mm lens, 1/2000 f4, ISO 200, RAW

Focal-Length Extension

Give the person who thought of this a medal for services to wildlife photography! Let's forget the technical reasons for it – the result is that most DSLRs multiply the focal length of your lens by a factor of between 1.2x and 1.6x. It may not be great for landscape photographers as their wide-angle lenses suddenly aren't wide-angle any more, but for animal snappers it is great as it provides the equivalent of a longer lens, allowing you to get close to animals without physically having to do so and without spending any extra money. Purrrrrr…fect.

Consistent Exposures

The DSLR provides a graphic histogram for each image. The histogram clearly shows whether an image is under- or overexposed or indeed if you've got it spot on. With experience, it is simple to interpret and this will be covered later (see p54). The histogram is a fantastic facility and, once you're familiar with it, will quickly become your best friend; when you've spent thousands of dollars on the trip of a lifetime what you want to come home with is a collection of great shots, and the histogram will help you achieve it. With experience, the histogram will allow you to achieve a near-perfect exposure every time without the need for light meters and so on – far too much hard work in the hectic world of the wildlife photographer.

Individual ISO Setting

The DSLR also gives another distinct advantage to the wildlife photographer. Because the digital sensors have greater sensitivity to light, you can continue shooting under light conditions that a film camera would find difficult if not impossible. The facility to alter the ISO or film speed on a shot-by-shot basis gives you superb flexibility and allows you

African elephant herd feeding, Masai Mara National Reserve, Kenya
One of the hidden benefits of a DSLR is the sensor's amazing sensitivity to light, especially once the rays of the sun have disappeared. This image, taken 20 minutes after sunset, shows amazing detail in the shadow areas straight out from the camera. The sensor has even picked out the moon – amazing.
▲ DSLR, 24-80mm lens, 1/60 f4, ISO 400, RAW

to change from ISO 100 to ISO 400 in, quite literally, the flick of a switch or dial. There's no need to fiddle about changing film and this will save you vital moments when your chosen subject has put in an appearance just as the sun has ducked below the horizon or a black cloud is passing overhead.

Confidence
The DSLR is a great confidence booster. Gone are the shackles of the cost of film; you are free to experiment, eliminate mistakes and hone your technique to your heart's content.

Digital Format – RAW Versus JPEG
The DSLR provides two different output formats – RAW and JPEG. The difference, which could run to the length of a steamy novel, boils down to flexibility and quality. A JPEG has the advantage of being viewable straight out of the camera. Shooting JPEG gives you more space in the camera's memory and thus a greater buffer size before lockout, and it also takes up less space on the memory card. The disadvantages are that it is compressed data (ie some detail has been eliminated to save space), it can show a lot more noise, and mistakes in exposure are not so easy to fix without specialist knowledge; for instance, if you muck up the white balance, it will be impossible to rectify. And because you can take more shots, you probably will, which can make editing a nightmare – you might end up with thousands of images from a single trip.

RAW files, on the other hand, contain all the image data, are easy to correct and edit using specialist software (such as RawShooter premium or Photoshop) and offer the optimum in quality. The disadvantage is that they use more data and so reduce buffer size and the number of images you can get on the memory card.

If you are travelling for a period of time, shooting JPEG will allow you to take far more pictures than shooting RAW. Unless you have many memory cards, it is useful to take along a portable downloading device such as a Jobo GigaVue to store the images from your cards in when you're out and about. By downloading your images to this temporary storage device, you can free your cards for reuse, making the choice of RAW versus JPEG a matter of personal preference. Having said that, to ensure maximum flexibility for the eventual output of your images, professional wildlife photographers always shoot RAW.

Compact Digital Cameras

One of the revolutions in photography over the past few years has been the emergence of the compact digital. All too often regarded as a camera for parties and family outings, the compact has come of age and is a great asset for the travelling wildlife photographer. The best models are armed with superb optical zooms in excess of 6x (equivalent to 300mm for a 35mm camera), support the RAW format, and have all manner of in-built filters, making them a valuable addition to your kit bag. With the addition of a built-in movie mode, these compact digital cameras offer a great alternative to the DSLR for the photographer who wants good quality with maximum flexibility and minimum weight. The main problem with them is that their rechargeable batteries have notoriously short lives; if you can get a model that takes off-the-shelf batteries then you will never regret buying one. Their only other disadvantage is the delay in shutter release from the press of the button, but with practice you can allow for this.

Sable antelope, Marwell Zoo, England
This image, taken in a zoological park in Hampshire, England, was made possible only by utilising the incredibly useful pop-out LCD screen of the compact digital. This made the low-angle composition very easy and the resulting image makes a very appealing A4 print that would compete against any DSLR.

▲ Compact digital, program mode, ISO 200, RAW

Underwater Cameras

Most of the natural world lies beneath the waves and to get out and experience this watery kingdom, you'll need to consider investing in a specialised underwater camera or an underwater housing for your existing one. There are various ways to make a camera waterproof. Several manufacturers make compact cameras that can be taken underwater to a depth of 5m, and for professionals Nikon makes a superb range of underwater SLRs. These days, however, the trend is to take your own compact or SLR underwater by packing it in a custom-designed waterproof housing. These housings vary in size and complexity but all allow you to look through the viewfinder and move all the normal controls via a series of levers and buttons. These housings are expensive, but they are the best tools for the job. Never be tempted to use a bag or a plastic housing – it's not worth the risk. Here are some tips on housings to help you on your way:

▸ **Maintenance** Small rubber seals called o-rings in the housings are what keep your camera dry. These seals are only effective if they are regularly cleaned and inspected for foreign bodies such as hairs, which could cause an expensive leak; your rings also have to be regularly greased. If in doubt consult an expert who will probably grease the rings for you.

▸ **Setup** Autofocus cameras work well underwater and have taken a lot of the guesswork out of underwater photography. An ISO 200 film with an f8 aperture is best as it will help account for any movement and give a decent depth of field.

▸ **DSLR Considerations** Load in the biggest memory card you have and make sure that you set the DSLR to RAW. Set the white balance to auto and the menu option to display the histogram after each exposure. This will allow you to check the exposure underwater without having to fiddle with a tiny switch. When you are photographing sharks or whales your attention is generally elsewhere!

▸ **Lighting** For most uses you will be snorkelling within a few feet of the surface and therefore can avoid the pain of using a flash. For deeper photography the water absorbs all colour and you will need some external light to restore it. In-camera flash units are able to penetrate a few feet of water, but if you need more then the only alternative is to use a specialist underwater unit. (For more information on underwater photography see Mark Webster's book, listed on p150). It's best to avoid using the flash altogether if you can help it.

Indian roller on territorial perch, Bandhavgarh National Park, India

Taken with a fixed 500mm lens, this picture shows one of the real benefits of such a fixed lens – a diffuse background. Coupled with a low aperture setting (see p52), this helps to isolate the subject and make a very simple yet striking image.

◂ 35mm SLR, 500mm lens, 1/250 f5.6, Velvia 50

LENSES

A good lens, perhaps more than anything else in your kit bag, will make a real difference to the quality of your final pictures. Lenses come in all shapes, sizes and prices and the choice can seem daunting. The one element that you cannot afford to scrimp on is a lens – there is no substitute for quality and it is always a false economy to buy the cheapest. In general, higher-priced lenses offer better optical quality, better low-light performance and much faster autofocus. It's also worth considering paying extra for lenses with image stabilisation. Many of the best telephoto lenses and long-range zooms are quite heavy and long in physical length. An image-stabilised lens reduces the risk of camera shake at low shutter speeds and makes hand-holding a long-range zoom in a bouncing boat or on a bumpy off-road drive an achievable reality. Don't forget to put lens hoods on all your lenses. A frequently ignored accessory, a lens hood will protect the lens against dust, insects and inclement weather.

The key for travelling wildlife photographers is to keep the lens choice simple and flexible. Good research before a trip will allow you to make the right choice and will pay dividends. For example, you will need different lenses for tracking tigers in India than you would for expedition cruising among the icebergs in Antarctica.

Telephoto Lenses

Telephoto lenses are those that are fixed in focal length; for example, 100mm, 200mm and 300mm. Your choice of lens will largely be determined by how close you intend to get to your chosen subject and how large you want it to be in the frame. A 100mm lens, for instance, is ideally suited to macrophotography, as it allows you to get close to small bugs and beasties, whereas a 300mm lens will allow you to focus in closely on an animal that is much further away – perhaps a leopard resting in a tree. Remember, the shorter the lens, the closer you will need to get to your subject for it to be full frame – a 100mm lens might not be the lens of choice when you're photographing that leopard then! The shorter lenses are particularly useful for taking images of animals in landscapes and habitats where you want to give a general impression of the area you are visiting, as they offer you great flexibility in how you compose your images. While telephoto lenses make it easier to get close to your subject, they can also increase camera shake, so you will need to use fast shutter speeds. It's best to use a shutter speed that is equivalent to, or faster than, the focal length of the lens, such as 1/250 for a 200mm lens.

Super Telephoto Lenses

For the professional or dedicated serious amateur working with very shy species in low light, the choice tends to be long, fixed-focal-length lenses in the 500–600mm range. For travel purposes, these lenses are hugely impractical, difficult to use and require specialist support. A lot of the time these lenses are overkill and, compositionally speaking, very limiting indeed. The issue of restricted composition applies equally to all fixed-focal-length lenses, as they allow you no framing options whatsoever – what you see is what you get.

Zoom Lenses

Zoom lenses are a different ball game and the ideal choice for the travelling wildlife photographer. They allow you to choose the composition you want and are much lighter than their fixed-focal-length cousins. A zoom lens is the ultimate in flexibility and you will be free to shoot and capture images in a wide range of situations. A zoom lens also has a hidden advantage for DSLR users; since you will not be changing the lens very frequently, the sensor will not be exposed to the hazards of dust. Choose a zoom with

Bald-eagle feathers, Alaska, USA

Typically opportunities present themselves when I am least ready. Having gone to visit a friend in the States, he took me to a rehabilitation centre for birds of prey, where I found this very accommodating bald eagle. Not having any macro gear with me, I simply attached an extension tube (see p21) onto my 100-400mm lens and ensured that I had a high enough depth of field for a nice, sharp image. Razor sharp, like my wit.

▲ DSLR, 100-400mm zoom lens, 1/60 f11, ISO 200 RAW, extension tube

an upper range of not less than 300mm, and ideally 400mm, as that will get you in the correct range for a decent shot of most wildlife. Attached to a DSLR, this 400mm upper range can become as high as 600mm (see p15) – a whopping range for any wildlife photographer.

For the really space- or weight-conscious traveller there are a few jack-of-all-trades zoom lenses which have incredible focal-length ranges that cover both wide-angle and long-range zooms, such as a 35–500mm lens. These lenses will struggle in low light with autofocus and you will have to trade a little in quality, but the flexibility required by many travelling photographers more than makes up for the disadvantages.

Wide-Angle Lenses

Some animals you will encounter are so friendly that you will quickly find a long-range zoom a little restrictive, not allowing you to tell the whole story with your pictures. When photographing penguins, for instance, or perhaps a herd of wildebeest sweeping majestically across the Kenyan plains, a good-quality wide-angle lens is a must. Try to choose one that doesn't overlap with the zoom too much and isn't too wide: a 24–70mm lens is a great combination and weighs virtually nothing. Although the primary purpose of your trip will be wildlife, you will no doubt find yourself in some beautiful locations and will want to·photograph the landscapes, people and culture, too. Versatility is as important to the travelling wildlife photographer as it is to the travel, landscape and people photographer.

Macro Lenses

If you are a plant or insect photographer, it is likely that you will have a specialist macro lens, usually a 50mm or 90mm. For everyone else, macrophotography is something that you want to try in a few situations, as and when the need arises or when you want to get closer to a subject than your existing lenses will allow. The first option is to ensure that your long-range zoom or wide angle has a macro or close-focus option, as this will be fine for most needs. If not, then an extension tube (a tube that sits between the camera and the lens) will magically transform your zoom lens into a close-focusing lens of microscopic proportions!

Teleconverters

Teleconverters are great accessories for lenses as they allow you to get increased magnification (usually 1.4x and 2x) for a fraction of the price of a new lens. The 1.4x is always a better option than the 2x, as the latter darkens the viewfinder image, slows down the

Orang-utan reaching for camera, Sepilok Rehabilitation Centre, Malaysia

A close encounter in a forest with a rehabilitated orang-utan called Christine led to this slightly offbeat image. Using a super wide-angle lens has accentuated the perspective, and a little fill-in flash has been used to lift the shadows in the face. In fact the only thing missing is the shot of the photographer wetting himself with laughter at having a tug of war with such an endangered yet endearing primate.

◀ 35mm SLR, 17-35mm lens, 1/60 f5.6, Sensia 100, flash

autofocus (if any) and loses two stops of light. Teleconverters are available for compact cameras, too, and can take the zoom into the 500mm range.

So that's the rucksack stuffed with cameras and lenses for all eventualities. Now let's see what else you might need.

Panther chameleon, Mantady National Park, Madagascar

Some creatures of this earth are so beautiful that they have to be taken in close-up to really do them justice. The amazingly diverse colours of this panther chameleon were irresistible to both the photographer and the naturalist in me. A 180mm macro allowed a close enough approach for a tight shot, without causing any stress to the chameleon, with a touch of flash to fill in the shadows.

▲ 35mm SLR, 180mm macro lens, 1/60 f11, Velvia 50, flash

Grizzly bear, Alaska, USA

Sometimes, it's best not to get closer to a subject than is absolutely necessary. Photographing mating grizzly bears in Alaska was one such time. My 500mm lens didn't get me quite close enough and moving in closer wasn't an option, not by the look this bear was giving me. My only option was to attach a teleconverter, which allowed me to take a few more steps towards the bear without moving a muscle.

◀ DSLR, 500mm lens with 1.4x teleconverter, 1/125 f5.6, ISO 100 RAW

FILTERS

For the wildlife photographer, the usage of filters is limited to two – the polariser and the 81A. The film user will use these filters a lot more than the DSLR photographer, who can replicate the effects in a RAW converter, which allows you to decide, from the comfort of your armchair, whether the image needs any more saturation or not. Be careful though, as it is easy to oversaturate a subject and make it a resident of Mars instead of Earth. DSLR owners should also be aware that unless you set your white balance to sunlight, the DSLR will compensate for the filter and negate its effect! For most DSLR photographers, a polarising filter is the only one whose effect cannot be replicated using software.

Don't take the cheap option for your filters either. Choose a high-quality glass filter such as those made by Lee Filters or B&W, because superior-quality glass does not come cheap. A cheap filter will be very noticeable on the quality of the resulting image and may ruin all the hard work you spent achieving it in the first place.

Polarising (PL) Filter

One filter that is invaluable for both the film and digital photographer is the polariser. This filter can drastically improve the impact of a blue sky or visibility through water. However, they are quite cumbersome, particularly the very best ones, as they require a custom mount and holder. You will also lose two stops of light when you use one, which means you could be shooting at a very low shutter speed and be prone to camera shake. Under the right conditions, however, the effect can be awesome.

Bottle-nosed dolphins, Honduras
Despite the beautiful blue-green hues of the tropical water, the equally tropical light is terrible at creating nasty reflections on the surface of the water. For images like this, I want to see the whole of the dolphin, or at least get an impression of it, so to cut through the glare off the water I used a polarising filter. An added benefit of using the filter is that it really enhances the blues of both the sea and sky, making the image both colourful and inviting.

▲ DSLR, 17-35mm lens, 1/125 f8, ISO 100 RAW, polarising filter

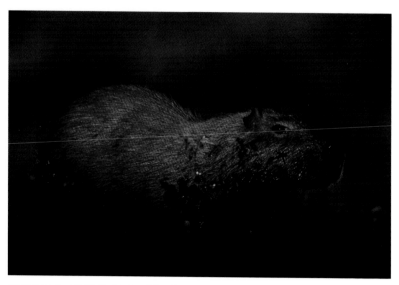

Capybara in last light, the Pantanal, Brazil

When I crept up to this capybara in the wetlands of the Pantanal, I quickly screwed an 81A filter onto the end of my lens, as I wanted to accentuate the red evening light that was just fading from the capybara's body. The result is far more representative of the image I saw than the camera would have otherwise recorded.

▲ 35mm SLR, 300mm lens, 1/60 f4, Provia 100F

81A Filter

The 81A filter is a warming filter that gives subtle warm tones to the overall image, helping to enhance the colour saturation of the image. Easy to use and great to give a boost to low, atmospheric light, it can be a handy filter to keep in your bag, especially if you are using film. The DSLR user rarely uses an 81A filter now as any RAW converter software can improve the saturation of an image in the same way. However, you still have to get the exposure right in the first place.

RAW Converter Filters

With the advent of digital technology and ever-improving RAW conversion software, you don't need to pack filters and wrap them carefully in tissue paper when using a DSLR. It is possible to experiment with a gamut of colour combinations to your heart's content when you are safely back home.

Red grouse, Northumberland, England
I had watched this displaying male red grouse from a small hillock for an hour through binoculars before crawling up to it. The late sun provided some nice saturation and I only needed to add a little tweak afterwards, using my RawShooter programme to further enhance it.
▲ DSLR, 300mm lens with 1.4x teleconverter, 1/180 f4, ISO 100 RAW

TRIPODS & OTHER SUPPORTS

It is a rare occurrence to photograph wildlife in strong, midday sunlight. Usually, animals are most active at the beginning or end of the day when the light is at its lowest and, from their point of view, its coolest. Correspondingly, this will reduce the shutter speed you will be shooting at, to areas below 1/250, which can lead to camera shake. Some form of extra support is needed, but one that suits a flexible, lightweight approach. The advice here is to research what you will need beforehand, how you will be shooting (eg hanging by a single hand from a runaway camel or from the comfort of a limousine) and then only take what is appropriate.

Light Tripod with Detachable Head

The traditional support for all areas of photography, tripods come in all shapes and sizes. Wildlife photographers rarely shoot standing up, as it either scares the subjects or, more

Common kingfisher, Hampshire, England

Shy creatures such as this stunning kingfisher require long hours of waiting patiently in a hide with only a dodgy novel for company. Holding a lens for this amount of time is simply impossible, so on this occasion I used a very robust carbon-fibre tripod to support my 500mm lens. For most hides a tripod works well, but for some you'll need to adopt a slightly more DIY approach and use a combination of clamps, tripod heads and strategically placed pieces of cardboard!

◀ DSLR, 500mm lens, 1/125 f8, ISO 100 RAW, tripod

Grey heron, Yala National Park, Sri Lanka

I took this backlit grey heron while using a specially designed car mount (clamp) from the side of my door. A car is the best form of hide, as wildlife is generally more used to vehicles than the horrific sight of yours truly in shorts. Note the space to the left of the image – this was deliberately done to balance the image and have the heron looking into the shot.

◄ DSLR, 500mm lens, 1/125 f5.6, ISO 100 RAW

alarmingly, makes them more aggressive and prone to snacking on humans. This means using a short tripod with a couple of extendable sections. A tripod made from carbon fibre or magnesium alloy will be very light to carry. When spread out low to the ground, the tripod will be very robust and able to keep a lens steady in quite a gust of wind. A high-set tripod just turns the lens into a tuneful wind instrument and all images will be blurred.

The second part of the tripod is the head. It is best to get a head that can be detached from the tripod. This will allow it to be used for other forms of support, such as clamps (see below). Try also to get a multipurpose head that can fulfil the needs of your longest lens and shortest wide-angle – a ball head will do just the job. Don't fret if you have a long telephoto lens such as a 500mm; try adding a Wimberley Sidekick to the ball head and you'll get amazing support for this beast of a lens.

Clamps

Clamps are very rarely used accessories. This is a shame as, when combined with a tripod head, they are a superb support device for working from the window or roof rack of the vehicle, especially on safari.

Beanbags

Beanbags are super flexible and fantastically useful bits of kit if you intend to shoot most of your pictures from a car or while balancing on a wall or some such object. Travelling completely flat and virtually weightless, they can be filled at your destination with all manner of dried beans, peas and even rice – whatever you can find locally (at a pinch they can even be stuffed with dirty socks). The top tip is to choose a double-walled beanbag, as this is able to grip the car window frame. Don't think that if you have a compact camera you cannot benefit from a beanbag; shake is an issue no matter which camera you use, so support is always helpful. Don't forget to responsibly dispose of your 'fillers' when you leave; beans, for instance, are often extremely welcome to local people and can supply them with food for months to come. Your socks may not be so welcome.

Juvenile cheetah, Masai Mara National Reserve, Kenya

I use beanbags probably more than I use a tripod. When working from a vehicle you have limited options to steady yourself. Beanbags are highly flexible and can allow you to balance on just about anything and are fantastic for leaning out of car windows or from the sunroof.

▲ DSLR, 100-400mm lens, 1/250 f5.6, ISO 100 RAW

FLASH UNITS

Flash is not as useful in wildlife photography as it is in other genres, simply because most animals you encounter will be terrified of it. There are some exceptions and, if correctly and ethically used, flash can create some beautiful highlights when used during the day and can provide vital illumination at night. Since a flash is lightweight and doesn't take up much room, it is a great accessory to take; the best choice is to pick one by the same manufacturer as your camera. The flash should have TTL (Through the Lens metering) capability, which allows the flash and camera to interact to get accurate exposures.

Off-Camera Bracket

If you plan to work at night, or with animals that have sensitive eyes (such as nocturnal animals), then you want at all costs to avoid attaching your flash to the camera hot shoe. This will cause the dreaded red eye, which has spoilt many a great picture. Instead, invest in an off-camera bracket that holds the flash either to one side or high above the camera. The flash fits on top and is connected to the hot shoe via a special TTL cord. The flash bracket may limit the angle at which you can shoot, but you'll soon be able to anticipate how the flash will light your subject.

Flash Extender

Sometimes you will need your flash to reach a lot further than its normal range; usually this is in conjunction with a long-focal-length lens. One solution is to buy a portable arc lamp and mount it on a truck, but a better solution is to use a flash extender. This is basically a plastic lens that fits onto the front of your flashgun to focus the beam and

Black panther, California, USA
An atmospheric, even sinister, image. To capture the scene at all, it was essential to use the flash. The dark clouds and approaching storm were looming and even using a flash extender I was lucky to get the shot before the heavens opened.

▲ 35mm SLR, 500mm lens, 1/60 f8, Provia 100F

Atlantic salmon jumping a waterfall, Highlands, Scotland
There are some situations where the contrast between the subject and the background is too great and the flash must be used to get anything meaningful. When I first saw salmon leaping this waterfall they were black dots against the blinding white torrent behind, so I used a single flash unit to light up the salmon without affecting the background. An amazing feat – not my getting the correct exposure, but the salmon's clearing such an obstacle in its final journey to spawn.

▲ DSLR, 70-200mm lens, 1/500 f5.6, ISO 100 RAW

extend its effective distance by several times. Best used in daylight, and always with an off-camera bracket, the extender will greatly improve images of birds and other animals in the rainforest canopy or those relaxing in the shade in the heat of the day. Best of all, it packs totally flat and will make no discernible difference to the weight of your rucksack.

Diffuser Cup

The diffuser cup is a plastic cup that fits over the end of your flashgun and will serve to cut down the power of the flash. This is an important point when photographing animals in dark situations, such as in a forest, or photographing animals that may be sensitive to the flash. Wildlife photographers are not paparazzi and have a responsibility not to harm or stress subjects in any way.

Second-Sync Flash

This is a reasonably difficult flash technique but can work well to create really atmospheric and artistic shots during daylight. Second-curtain synchronisation (also known as rear-curtain sync) basically means that the flash goes off when the curtain in the camera closes, not when it opens, as is the case in the normal use of a flash. The setting can be found either on the camera's custom function menu or on the flash. It is a great technique for creating motion trails in a moving image, leading to or from the subject, and can allow you to convey a sense of movement in your image instead of the usual goal of freezing that all-important moment in time. Used in conjunction with a slow shutter speed, it is wonderful for creating distinctive images.

Crowned lemur, Parc National des Tsingy de Bemaraha, Madagascar
Given lemurs generally live in dark rainforests, they have very sensitive eyes, so I used an off-camera bracket with a diffuser cup over the flash. At the expense of reducing the effective range, this softens the output, which is great for the subject and photographer alike – you can see how cool the lemur is about having his picture taken!

▲ 645 SLR, 300mm lens, 1/60 f5.6, Fuji Velvia 50, flash

Lar gibbon, Khao Yai National Park, Thailand

Using a second-sync flash is an option that's set either on the camera's custom functions or the flash itself. Just set a slow shutter speed and try it out – you may get some amazing results.

◀ 35mm SLR, 70-200mm lens with 1.4x teleconverter, 1/60 f8, Provia 100F, flash

CAMERA BAGS

Camera bags are often not given much consideration, but they are as vital as every other accessory described in this section, as they protect and transport your valuable gear. The best and most practical bag for the travelling wildlife photographer is the photographic rucksack: it is light, made to take the rigours of travel and carries a surprising amount of gear. It also allows you to walk and work with your cameras securely on your back while also keeping both hands free to hold and operate a camera. The best ones have waterproof covers and are ergonomically designed for comfort. Some of these harnesses wouldn't be out of place at the top of Everest but can also fit into airline baggage compartments. When choosing a rucksack for the job, pick one that is too big for your current amount of gear, as it will not be long before you grow into it. Don't buy one that has room for a laptop, unless you travel and really need it, because laptops are not made for the rigours of outdoor life!

Gannet preening its feathers, Bass Rock, Scotland

Working on offshore islands is a fantastic experience, especially when you see birds as beautiful as this gannet. But it can be painful if you don't have the right bag, as your shoulders certainly feel it by the end of the day.

▲ 35mm SLR, 300mm lens, 1/80 f11, Velvia 50

Japanese crane displaying, Hokkaido, Japan

Sometimes a good rucksack saves not only your back and shoulders. On this trip I broke my tripod and had to use the rucksack on the ground as a glorified beanbag, which gave my Japanese colleagues a great laugh.

▲ 35mm SLR, 500mm lens, 1/640 f5.6, Provia 100F

ACCESSORIES

By now your rucksack will probably be getting rather full, but there is sure to be some room to cram in a few extra accessories that may come in very useful one day.

Angle Finder

An angle finder is a useful little gizmo that fits onto the camera's viewfinder and looks like a miniature periscope. It allows the camera to be flat on the ground without you having to be, which is great for those tuxedo-wearing photographers out there. It is also a must-have for all macro photographers, as it means you can get your camera close to your subject without bending double to get your eye near the viewfinder. The other great thing about the angle finder is that it comes compete with a rubber eyecup, which cuts out light and other distracting things in your peripheral vision.

Remote Trigger Devices

A fun thing to try is to put your camera down in a likely spot and trigger it remotely. Many custom-made devices can be purchased for less than the price of a Porsche's wing mirror. However, there are two drawbacks to this kind of photography. The first is the need to change film after 36 shots or the memory card when it is full. Your subject may not be too pleased about this and your photography is likely to be reduced to a single film or card. A DSLR is a real advantage with this kind of photography, as a decent-sized card can hold hundreds of images, thus maximising your chances of getting the shot you want. The second problem is that your camera will become interesting to all and sundry and at best will be scent-marked by an animal. At worst it will be crushed before your eyes!

Wild boar, Bavaria, Germany

I love getting down in the dirt, but sometimes even I draw the line at a mouthful of mud or even worse – natural fertiliser! I used an angle finder, with a super wide-angle lens, to get this in-habitat shot of a wild boar in the middle of a forest, thus making sure it was only my knees and tripod legs that were covered in muck!

▲ 35mm SLR, 17-35mm lens, 1/60 f11, Velvia 50

Guira cuckoos after morning wash, the Pantanal, Brazil

If it hadn't been for regular scanning of the environment with a pair of binoculars, I would have never seen this shot of a group of Guira cuckoos. Since they tended to sit in a very distracting habitat, I used a long-focal-length lens and a low aperture to isolate them from the messy background.

▲ 35mm SLR, 600mm lens with 1.4x teleconverter, 1/60 f5.6, Velvia 50

Tool Kit & Multipurpose Knife

Cameras and lenses are not built for the rigours of travel and have lots of tiny screws that can easily come loose and stop a vital function from working. A couple of jewellers' screwdrivers and a multipurpose knife will sort you out in most circumstances. Don't forget that these will have to travel in your hold baggage during air travel.

Binoculars

Vitally important for most wildlife-spotting is a pair of good binoculars. These will greatly increase your enjoyment of your trip and enable you to locate and observe your subject from some distance away. A pair in the range of 10 x 42 will be perfect for the job, but make sure they are reasonably small and light to carry.

Inquisitive wild dog, private game reserve, South Africa

Using your camera remotely can give you a unique perspective on the animal world. I sometimes use this technique, particularly with shy creatures. Be warned though: you must be prepared to lose your valuable equipment. This little darling took the camera in its jaws and crushed the transmitter unit; that is what you call an expensive shot. Fortunately I was able to recover the film, complete with teeth marks!

◀ DSLR, 17-35mm lens, 1/250 f5.6, ISO 100 RAW

FILM & DIGITAL MEDIA

Equally important to the type of camera and lenses that you use is the format in which you capture your images – the 'medium'. This refers to the type of film (or digital equivalent) you prefer to use. There is a myriad of choices, all of which will essentially lead you to the same place: getting that great wildlife shot.

FILM

A common theme running through this book is flexibility, and this is especially crucial when you're choosing the right film to take. As a wildlife photographer you will inevitably face adverse weather conditions and have to shoot in all kinds of light levels, so you need a film that can cope with everything. Sadly, this has not yet been invented, but a good compromise is to take along a good supply of very fine-grain ISO 100 film, which can easily be 'pushed' to ISO 200 in poor light. Slow films generally have a finer grain than fast films, so if you're looking for lots of clarity and detail in your images, then a fine-grain film is best. Remember to put a permanent marker pen in your bag to highlight the films that have been pushed, as they will need to be processed separately. One final tip is to take far more film than you think you will need, as you are very likely to use it and will curse yourself if you run out. Buying film on location can be difficult, and dodgy out-of-date film that has sat on a baking hot shelf covered by insects will do little for your end results or your wallet.

DIGITAL MEDIA

Here we break the flexibility rule. The only rule when considering digital media is to take as many memory cards as you can afford to buy! If you are away for a few weeks, it will be amazing how many pictures you will take. Even if you have a portable downloader, you will need at least three high-capacity memory cards to cater for the times when that giant panda is performing cartwheels in front of you. Try to get cards with at least two GB in capacity (especially if you are shooting RAW) and don't waste your money on 'high-performance' cards that promise the earth in terms of performance. These cards are expensive and you will not notice any discernible difference; it is better to buy a recognised brand. Some DSLRs have slots for two cards, generally a CF and an SD (secure digital), so if your DSLR provides this capability, take advantage of it and have every slot crammed with every byte of storage you can.

DIGITAL ACCESSORIES

If you are a DSLR owner and on anything longer than an overnight trip, you will have to consider the issue of image storage. At some stage all of your memory cards will fill up and you will need to offload them safely in order to free them up for more award-winning pictures. There are two options to help you solve this dilemma – the laptop and the portable downloader. The downloader is a portable hard drive that fits in the palm of your hand, usually with a good screen and a slot that can take several different types of memory card. Downloaders come in various sizes, from 40 GB upwards, and the best come with external battery packs and car chargers. The great advantages of the downloader are its size, portability and durability; it is also designed solely for the task at hand. Although

Jaguar in rainforest, Belize
◀ 35mm SLR, 500mm lens, 1/100 f5.6, Provia 100F

a laptop can be used to store images, it is fragile and heavy and can be a real burden in remote locations. A laptop is also a device designed for the business environment, not for sitting around a campfire. Not only may it cause you difficulties in being able to access sufficient or correct power, but you are also more likely to become a target for thieves. Choose a downloader: it is the only suitable device for the job and will fit nicely into that final slot in your rucksack.

Red deer stag at sunset, the Highlands, Scotland

All photographers learn by experience; it is one way that we improve our photography and keep challenging ourselves. Late one afternoon I had been stalking this stag and as luck would have it, it was walking right into my shot just as the last rays of sun lit it with a beautiful red light. I took a couple of shots, then pressed the shutter again but got no response. The memory card was full. Arggggggggghhhh! Thinking quickly, I deleted a couple of earlier shots of some nameless small brown bird and managed to get this one before filling up the card again. A vital lesson – don't scrimp on cards.

▲ DSLR, 300mm lens with 1.4x teleconverter, 1/60 f4, ISO 200 RAW

African elephant, Waterberg, South Africa

It is all too easy to underestimate just how many images you will take, especially as a travelling wildlife photographer. By always erring on the side of caution and taking too much film or digital storage space, you'll be sure to never run out of opportunities to capture the myriad once-in-a lifetime opportunities that will come your way.

▲ 35mm DSLR, 300mm f4L lens, 1/250 f6.3, ISO 100 RAW

PART TWO

TECHNICAL ELEMENTS

Before you get too excited and board that flight to Timbuktu, take a few days to practise and revise your basic photographic technique so that you will be confident when it really matters – in the field. Whether you are shooting the friendliest wildlife in the world or the rarest and most elusive, you still need to understand basic techniques to get shots that do the situation and yourself justice. With wildlife you often do not have time to carefully calculate exposure, set depths of field and such like – it's often a case of shooting from the hip. To assist you, here's a no-nonsense guide to getting it right first time and a basic grounding for those trickier photo techniques.

Rockhopper penguin taking a freshwater shower, Falkland Islands
◄ DSLR, 70-200mm lens, 1/125 f8, ISO 100 RAW, flash

EXPOSURE

Exposure is a complex subject and what follows is a very short explanation to refresh your memory while you travel. It applies equally to film and DSLR users, although the specifics of DSLR exposure are dealt with on p54. Exposure is analogous to watering the garden. Think of your film as a garden, and the lens and shutter as a tap. The longer you turn on the tap, the more water will get through. This is the shutter speed, and it determines how long the film is exposed to light. If you have a very thin hose, it will take you longer to water the garden than if you have a wide fire hose. Thus, the wider the opening in the lens (the aperture), the more light can travel through. The quality of light used to expose the film is similar to the water pressure behind the hose. Midday sunlight is very strong, while an indoor tungsten globe produces light of a relatively low intensity. Moonlight is softer still.

Your camera uses a combination of two linear measurements – aperture and shutter speed – to interpret how much light is needed to get the correct exposure. The aperture is controlled by the lens and is a measure of how wide the lens iris is set, while the shutter speed is a measure of how much time light is allowed to fall on the film or sensor for.

EXPOSURE RATIO

Think of the aperture as the hose that varies the 'flow' of light reaching the film or sensor. If you want more light then you choose a wider aperture (or hose) or leave the shutter (the

Pink-backed pelicans, Chobe National Park, Botswana
Choosing the right exposure ratio can make a huge difference to a picture. When I first took a meter reading from these two pelicans, the camera's light meter gave me a reading of 1/640 at f5.6. I knew from experience, however, that as both pelicans were not quite parallel to me (the adult on the right was slightly closer), an aperture of f5.6 would not give enough depth of field to get them both in focus. I decided f8 would be a better bet, and this gave a new shutter speed of 1/320, thus maintaining the exposure ratio. In other words, changing the aperture to f8 let less light into the camera, and the shutter compensated for this by staying open longer.
▲ DSLR, 17-35mm lens, 1/320 f8, ISO 100 RAW

Black rhinoceros, Waterberg, South Africa
◀ DSLR, 500mm lens, 1/125 f5.6, ISO 100 RAW, tripod

White-tailed sea eagle, western coast, Norway

Flight shots are one genre where it is very important to get the correct exposure ratio. Initially, you might think that all that matters is shooting at a fast shutter speed to freeze the motion, but equally vital is the aperture to get a good depth of field and therefore the whole bird in sharp focus. For this I used an aperture of f8, which still gave me a shutter speed of 1/500 – perfect for stopping the motion of the eagle.

◀ DSLR, 500mm lens, 1/500 f8, ISO 200 RAW

tap) open for a longer time. This increases the amount of light (the water) reaching the film or sensor and decreases the amount of time needed to reach the perfect exposure. As both the aperture and shutter speed are related to the exposure, any change in aperture must produce a corresponding change in shutter speed to keep everything in balance. From the tap analogy you can see that although there is only one correct exposure, there can be many combinations of shutter speed and aperture to give this value. The combination of shutter speed and aperture is called the exposure ratio. For example 1/125 at f5.6 has the same exposure ratio as 1/500 at f2.8, although the effects of each will be very different indeed (see p49 and p52).

All cameras, whether SLR or compact digital, have program modes that are designed to give you a starting point for the exposure ratio. These all have a slightly different bias; for example, aperture priority (AV) allows you to set the aperture while the camera adjusts the shutter speed to keep the same exposure ratio. From a practical standpoint it is best to stick to a single program mode and get used to how it works; AV is this author's recommendation.

You didn't think it was as simple as that, did you? Unfortunately it's not, as the camera's built-in light meter has other ideas. It is not really the light meter's fault: it just expects everything to be a neutral shade of grey and few things in nature ever are. So, to make amends, it tries to compensate by giving you an exposure based on the neutral tones, ie grey. This is why black subjects are generally overexposed and white subjects are usually far too dark. Using fewer metering points (a tighter metering pattern) exacerbates the situation, as there are fewer colours for the camera to use to create a realistic judgement. This is one reason why most professionals use a wide metering pattern rather than spot metering.

EXPOSURE COMPENSATION

Leaving the light meter to its own devices is clearly not a good idea in most cases. The exposure value it gives must be considered as a starting point only and viewed with a degree of mistrust. In fact, you will often need to override the exposure and adjust either the shutter speed or the aperture to compensate for the light-meter inaccuracy. Note: this is different from merely adjusting a program mode to get a different exposure ratio; if an exposure of 1/250 at f5.6 is wrong, then adjusting it to 1/125 at f8 will still be wrong. One or other of the values must be adjusted to override the exposure ratio (eg 1/250 at f8), and this is called exposure compensation. Most cameras have this facility either via a button marked +/- or a large rear thumbwheel. Compact cameras have this facility too, although on some models it is slightly hidden as a function of the main menu. Knowing when to compensate and how to do it is the real trick, and Part 3 (p97) will deal with some practical realities and how to get the best exposure results in the field without wasting hundreds of shots.

African leopard, private game reserve, South Africa
In some situations the camera light meter can be trusted almost completely; here, in the beautiful soft morning light, there are no visible extremes of colour (black or white) in the shot to fool it.
▲ DSLR, 70-200mm lens with 1.4x teleconverter, 1/125 f5.6, ISO 100 RAW

Arctic wolf, Canada

White subjects, or white backgrounds for that matter, cause the light meter to underexpose the image. Shooting white subjects in overcast conditions as shown will *always* give better results than glaring sunlight. As a rule of thumb, white subjects, or those with white backgrounds, always need to have a little positive-exposure compensation applied, in the range of +½ to +1½ stops.

▲ 35mm SLR, 500mm lens with 1.4x teleconverter, 1/250 f4.5 (+½ stop compensated from f5.6), Provia 100F

**Tufted duck,
Surrey, England**

There are always some awkward subjects and this tufted duck has both ends of the spectrum present in its plumage. Sensible thought would indicate that the light meter would take an average of the two and get it right. If only life were so simple. It depends entirely upon which metering pattern is in use and the percentage of each colour. Don't worry – situations like this are easy to expose, using the constant-tones technique described on p57.

▲ 35mm SLR, 600mm lens, 1/250 f5.6, Provia 100F

WORKING WITH SHUTTER SPEED

Shutter speed is used to control how you want a moving subject to appear, ie either razor sharp or blurred. To get a razor-sharp image you choose a high shutter speed (generally 1/500 and above), whereas anything under 1/60 will begin to give you a blurred effect. Very few photographers use slow shutter speeds, but in the right hands this intentionally blurred effect can really enhance the image. When using slow shutter speeds, remember that the two parameters of shutter speed and aperture are inextricably linked. As the

Kingfisher erupting with fish, Oxfordshire, England
High-action situations such as this demand really high shutter speeds, which can only be obtained with the fastest lenses and brightest light conditions.

▲ DSLR, 70-200mm lens, 1/8000 f4, ISO 400 RAW

Little egrets fighting, Yala National Park, Sri Lanka
Usually most action can be stopped by using a shutter speed of 1/1000 sec. With a DSLR this is easy to achieve, even in low light, by increasing the ISO setting. This will also increase the noise in the final image, but this can easily be reduced in RawShooter.

◀ DSLR, 300mm lens with 1.4x teleconverter, 1/1000 f4, ISO 100 RAW

shutter speed is reduced, the aperture must increase to compensate for this. Increasing the aperture will bring more of the background into focus, which might be distracting in certain situations, so watch out for this.

A hidden benefit of keeping the shutter speed as high as possible is that it will minimise the chance of you accidentally ruining your images because of camera shake. A shutter speed any slower than 1/30 is likely to lead to camera shake. This is an important consideration when working in areas where a tripod is impractical, such as on the back seat of a car or when riding an elephant. If you don't have a tripod, it's a good idea to hold your breath while taking the photo and find something against which you can support either yourself or the camera.

Great black-backed gull flying, western coast, Norway
I'd taken a lot of images of the gulls flying, but looking on the LCD the composition wasn't really doing it for me. So I selected a much lower shutter speed, highlighted all the autofocus points, used servo/tracking autofocus and a technique called panning. Keeping my legs still and my eye firmly in the viewfinder, I moved my upper body to track the motion of the gull, shooting continuously while I was moving. This continuous motion while shooting creates the streaks that you see here and is a great technique for creating more interesting images.

▾ DSLR, 70-200mm lens with 1.4x teleconverter, 1/20 f11, ISO 50 RAW

Spotted deer running, Yala National Park, Sri Lanka

The panning technique (see below) works well with mammals when they are moving quickly. In this case I used it to create an interesting shot and take attention away from a distracting foreground and background.

▲ DSLR, 70-200mm lens with 1.4x teleconverter, 1/30 f16, ISO 100 RAW

Golden plover, Northumberland, England

A slower shutter speed can also be used to great effect when taking more static subjects, as these may occasionally provide a chance movement or behaviour that can be accentuated through blurring. Shooting in this manner I was able to capture part of the courtship display of this golden plover which might have been overlooked by the casual observer or photographer.

◀ 35mm DSLR, 500mm lens with 1.4x teleconverter, 1/125 f5.6, ISO 200 RAW

WORKING WITH APERTURE

The lens aperture controls the depth of field, ie how much of the image is in focus. Low apertures, such as from f4 to f5.6, are generally used to isolate the subject from the background, perhaps for an intimate portrait. At higher apertures, much more of the background detail comes into sharp focus, which can be a little distracting for some wildlife images, as animals are not always found in picturesque locations. For most situations, the highest aperture that wildlife photographers will need to shoot is around f16 for a nice 'animal in habitat' shot; however, at this aperture the effect of reduced shutter speed and camera shake (p50) may well come into play, so watch out.

Also useful for SLR users is the 'depth of field preview' button, which is usually located close to the SLR or DSLR lens mount (compacts do not tend to have this function). The button allows you to see a slightly darkened (by one stop) image through the viewfinder. By adjusting the aperture, you can assess its effect on the depth of field of your image and determine whether there is too much of the background in focus or not enough.

Black-browed albatross chick on nest, Falkland Islands

These images clearly show the effect of different apertures. The image on the left was shot at f4, while the one on the right was shot at f22. At f4 there is just an impression of the background and the focus of the picture is the chick; at f22 the background becomes equally important and the focus is on the 'chick in habitat'.

▲ DSLR, 70-200mm lens, 1/2000 f4 and 1/60 f22, ISO 100 RAW

Spotted hyena, Chobe National Park, Botswana

This simple shot of a hyena looking intently at a possible meal was taken in beautiful red morning light. To concentrate the viewer on the hyena I used a low aperture to ensure the background was nice and diffuse.

▲ 35mm SLR, 600mm lens, 1/125 f5.6, Velvia 50

Timber wolf, Montana, USA

A tricky picture to assess. I wanted to get good facial detail (sharp from nose to ears) and give an impression of the background without it being overpowering. Too low an aperture would cause elements of the face (the nose and eyes) to lose their sharpness, too high and the background would be distracting. In a situation like this, I use the depth-of-field preview function. The viewfinder image will be stopped down (made darker by one stop) and you will be able to increase the aperture and see the effect that each setting has on the subject and background. DSLR photographers can use the LCD screen for this too.

◀ 35mm SLR, 100-400mm lens, 1/125 f8, Provia 100F

THE DSLR & EXPOSURE

There is no doubt that the DSLR makes getting the correct exposure much easier than a film camera does, as a certain element of guesswork has been removed. However, the DSLR still requires that you understand the basics of exposure as it can be very unforgiving if you over- or underexpose the image.

All DSLRs, and most compact digitals, provide a histogram on their LCD display that will tell you if the image is over-, under- or correctly exposed. At first glance it looks impossibly difficult to understand, but it is in fact remarkably simple. The left axis shows the black pixels in the image, the central axis indicates the average tone that most light meters strive towards (neutral or grey tones), and the right axis shows the white pixels in the image. The simple rule for histograms is to keep the average peak of the image right on the centre line, or slightly to the left. The latter is particularly important when shooting images that have a lot of highlights or white subjects or backgrounds (eg snow or looking up into

Black-browed albatross, Falkland Islands

One of the world's most stunning birds, the albatross has the distinction of giving an LCD histogram that looks like a mountain range because of its black and white plumage. Keeping the majority of the peaks slightly to the left of the centre line, I avoided overexposing the white areas of the image. This, however, was my secondary consideration when taking the image – trying not to fall off the precipitous cliff she was nesting on came first!

▲ DSLR, 300mm lens, 1/500 f8, ISO 100 RAW

trees), as the DSLR tends to burn out any highlights. Burnout means that the camera will not record any detail in that section of the image and the resulting 'bright' area can make an otherwise great image look unsightly. It is that simple. The perfectly exposed image with a spread of colours will have a uniform bell-shaped curve peaking around the centre line, but that rarely occurs in reality.

African white-backed vulture, Masai Mara National Reserve, Kenya

I took this picture of a vulture with the light meter compensated to −2/3 stop (the Rouse method; see p58). Checking the LCD histogram showed that most of the peaks were just to the left of the centre line, a perfect exposure to ensure that the white of the feathers was not burnt out.

◀ DSLR, 70-200mm lens, 1/2000 f4, ISO 100 RAW

FIELD EXPOSURE GUIDE

The Holy Grail for all camera manufacturers is to develop a light meter that gives great results in all situations without any user intervention. So far, this is still a dream, although the DSLR histogram at least tells you when you have it wrong so that you can correct it in the field. The three images below show the three different methods that can be used to get a starting point for your exposure without worrying about the colour or tone of your subject. This section is still relevant to DSLR users because even though the LCD histogram will give you another chance to get it right your subject may not!! It always pays to get the exposure right first time.

Neutral-Point Method

In most pictures there will be a neutral or medium-toned object, such as a tree (as in the pine marten image) or a rock. Neutral or medium toned simply means that it does not have extremes of colour, ie black or white. Provided that this object is in the same light as the subject, simply frame it in the viewfinder and take a light reading. If your camera has an exposure-lock capability, lock the exposure in, recompose the shot and bingo, the exposure will be pretty much spot on. If you cannot lock the exposure, try entering the manual-program mode and dial in both values (shutter speed and aperture) – a method that will rarely let you down.

Constant-Tones Method

Another trick that professionals use if they do not have a neutral point is to twist the lens focus to either infinity or its closest focal point. This renders the viewfinder image

Pine marten, the Highlands, Scotland

The pine marten is a very quick and unpredictable creature to photograph, as it is always on the move. There simply wasn't time to expose on the animal itself when it appeared. I used the neutral-point method here and exposed on the tree bark before the animal emerged, which basically made the difference between getting the shot and not.

◀ 35mm SLR, 100-400mm lens, 1/250 f5.6, Provia 100F

Young great grey owl, Repovesi National Park, Finland

I could have used the neutral-point method here but chose instead to use the constant-tones method of exposing the image, as I wasn't sure how the blacks in the feathers would affect the exposure and felt that this would be more reliable.

◀ DSLR, 300mm lens, 1/320 f2.8, ISO 100 RAW

Harp seal pup sleeping, Îles de la Madeleine (Magdalen Islands), Canada
With a distinct lack of neutral tones in this image, the neutral-point method was out. The constant-tones method would have been a good starting point but the best exposure was given by the sunny f16 rule. With lots of practice, instinct took over, which saved me a lot of worry when I was more concerned about my fingers dropping off in the subzero temperatures.

▲ 35mm SLR, 17-35mm lens, 1/320 f8, Velvia 50

completely blurred and out of focus, which usually removes the distracting extremes of colour and helps the meter make a better (and more accurate) choice for the exposure. In the great grey owl example on p57, the background is already nice and diffuse and very neutral in colour. The previous method could be used here as well, as both the owl and the post are neutral tones.

The F16 Rule

The f16 rule says that on a sunny day with the sun directly over your shoulder the exposure will be 1/125 at f16 on ISO 100 film. Using exposure ratios, this equates to 1/250 at f11, 1/500 at f8 etc. Use this as a starting point and underexpose slightly, particularly if you have a DSLR. It sounds complicated but it just takes practise. Needless to say, the DSLR histogram makes it all a lot easier.

DSLR Exposure – The Rouse Method

Unfortunately, most wildlife encounters are very short and you will not have time to spend on calculating your exposures. If you are using a film camera, you will need to become very experienced at judging when the light meter has it wrong. DSLR users, however, can relax and use the Rouse method. Simply set the exposure compensation to –2/3 stop, ie 2/3 stop underexposed. Generally, the DSLR tends to overexpose, so this method ensures that you will always have slightly underexposed images. You can then use a RAW converter such as RawShooter premium to make any necessary adjustments to the exposure, which may be as much as two stops in some cases, without any signifi-cant degradation to the image. (JPEG shooters note that you can still try this method, but your adjustments will have to be made in an image-editor program). This method works for a wide variety of situations and is a great starting point; if you have the time, use the LCD histogram to fine-tune it to get a histogram slightly to the left of centre.

Giant panda feeding, Wolong Reserve, China

I liked the way that the panda was playing with the bamboo and waving it from side to side. To capture it effectively, I used the flash and combined it with a slow shutter speed of 1/30, which created the motion blur. An off-camera bracket removed the chance of red eye, while a flash extender made sure that the light reached the distant panda.

▲ 35mm SLR, 500mm lens, 1/30 f11, Provia 100F, flash

Flash Exposure

If you are using flash in daylight, you only want to brighten the shadows and to have little or no effect on the overall exposure. Therefore, a good starting point is to set the compensation on the flash unit to −2 stops; for slightly older flashguns without this facility, simply set the ISO to two settings below the ISO rating that you are using for the camera. For example, if you have set the camera to ISO 100, then setting the flash to ISO 400 will achieve the required effect. This rule applies equally if you are using a flash extender, as the power from the flash unit is concentrated and will need to be reduced.

When using flash at night, the best approach is to put the camera and flash on full automatic and let them work it all out. If you have a DSLR, you will need to reduce the flash exposure by as much as −1 stop, as the DSLR sensor is incredibly sensitive to flashlight. A RAW converter may be able to perform miracles with exposure but it cannot replace detail that has been burnt out of the picture by the flash.

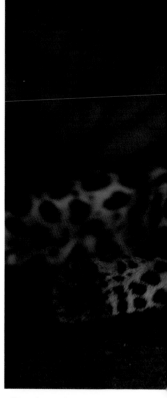

African leopard, MalaMala Game Reserve, South Africa

One trick to give your flash pictures a better appearance at night is to use an external light to provide the main illumination. This is a common trick on safari; here the light was plugged into the cigarette lighter of the car. Since the light level is quite high, the flash does not have to put out much light, so your batteries last longer and you get a much warmer-looking picture without having to fiddle with the white balance or put on special filters.

▲ DSLR, 300mm lens, 1/125 f5.6, ISO 400 RAW, flash

Badger hanging down to drink, Hampshire, England
Special brackets are available that use two flashguns to give a slightly better coverage for the flash and remove some of the harsh shadows associated with a single flash. Although it was a nightmare hanging down the bank while keeping both units pointing at the badger and not letting myself fall into the water, the effort was well worth it, as it is a very different badger shot from the norm.

◀ 35mm SLR, 70-200mm lens, 1/60 f11, Ektachrome 100, flash

COMPOSITION

One area of photography where opinions have always varied has been the subject of composition. There are various rules that are bandied about in books – the rule of thirds, having threes etc, but in general these are just opinions and there is no hard and fast rule. The bottom line is that if you like it, and it works for you, then it is a great composition. There are, however, some suggestions that may help.

Grizzly bear on log, Alaska, USA

A very simple composition, placing the bear to the right of the image, has it looking into the picture, giving the picture space to breathe.

▲ DSLR, 500mm lens, 1/500 f4, ISO 200 RAW

Red squirrel, Scotland

Sometimes, the natural posture of an animal dictates how you are able to shoot and compose a particular image. This red squirrel's major feature is its tail, which adopts a vertical position. Naturally, the best composition for this upright position is a vertical one, leading the eye diagonally across the image.

◀ 35mm DSLR, 70-200mm lens, 1/125 f5.6, ISO 200 RAW

Black grouse, Northumberland, England

◀ DSLR, 300mm lens with 1.4x teleconverter, 1/60 f4, ISO 100 RAW, beanbag

THE 'BULL'S-EYE'

When in doubt, just centre the image in the frame; this is called a bull's-eye. It is the quickest and easiest composition. Again, choose f5.6 or f8 to get good subject sharpness while keeping the background diffuse.

Bald eagle, Homer, USA
I just wanted the focus to be on the eagle so I positioned the eye slightly to the right of the centre line to create a very simple yet striking image.

▲ DSLR, 100-400mm lens, 1/125 f8, ISO 50 RAW

Tree anteater, Belize

Tree anteaters live in very thick forest and this chap was in a particularly thick tree. I had no choice but to put the body dead centre, as a very distracting tree was just to the left of the head and would have ruined the soft tones of the picture. I put the autofocus point right over the anteater's eye and used a fixed-focal-length lens at a low aperture to keep the background out of focus.

◀ 35mm SLR, 70-200mm lens with 1.4x teleconverter, 1/60 f4, Provia 100F

Wild goat, the Highlands, Scotland

Sometimes having a fixed-focal-length lens is a blessing, sometimes a nightmare. On this occasion I had gently eased myself down a muddy bank for over an hour to get close to this chap, only to find that he came so close to investigate me that I could barely fit him in the frame. So I slowly turned the camera to the vertical, put the autofocus point right between his eyes and trusted the exposure meter as the tones were pretty neutral.

▲ 35mm SLR, 300mm lens, 1/125 f5.6, Velvia 50

ORIENTATION

Knowing how to format the image is a skill that only comes with practice. Most of us naturally hold the camera in a horizontal (landscape) position so it follows that most images that we take are in this format – besides, all the buttons and writing suggest it should be so. Turning the camera on its side to shoot portrait format does require conscious thought, which in the excitement of the shoot is nearly always forgotten. However, portrait format does suit a multitude of situations – particularly intimate portraits or bird photography, where the subject is usually portrait shaped.

Burchell's zebra foal, Masai Mara National Reserve, Kenya

Shooting with my 500mm, the only option was to use portrait format, as landscape format would have left no space above or below the foal and would have chopped the mother's body in half.

◀ DSLR, 500mm lens, 1/500 f5.6, ISO 100 RAW

Waxwing on perch, Repovesi National Park, Finland

Another example of a picture that works well in both formats. Portrait style would have given slightly more space above the head, but I wanted to show more of the branch leading out from the image, so landscape format was the final choice. My main concern was keeping the background diffuse, as it was someone's red garden fence!

▲ DSLR, 500mm lens, 1/125 f5.6, ISO 100 RAW

Gentoo penguin in sandstorm, Falkland Islands

Sometimes a picture works well in both formats and it is the composition that determines which is the best to use. Here the penguin is walking into the empty area on the left of the image, which helps to give the image space and lets me show the environment as well as the penguin's struggle against it.

▲ DSLR, 300mm lens, 1/60 f8, ISO 100 RAW

European bison, Białowieża Forest, Poland

Big mammals like this bison present great problems when trying to decide the correct format. Unless you can include the whole of the body and leave space around the head, the only choice is to try for a portrait head shot. A good tip is to use an animal's shoulder to lead in from one corner to create a natural path for your eye to follow when looking at the shot.

◀ 35mm SLR, 500mm lens with 1.4x teleconverter, 1/250 f5.6, Provia 100F

FOCUS

Focus is the vital ingredient to any photographic image of the natural world (unless, of course, it is intentionally blurred for artistic reasons). An out-of-focus shot should be consigned to the bin regardless of how stunning the subject or situation was. Getting images in focus comes with practice and is something everyone gets wrong from time to time. However, there are several ways to minimise the chance of error.

Autofocus has revolutionised wildlife photography, bringing seemingly impossible high-action shots within reach of even the most budget-priced SLR. Autofocus systems do vary depending on the manufacturer, and some are clearly better than others, but *any* autofocus system will benefit your wildlife photography. The key to using it effectively is to learn how it works and to keep on top of it at all times; relying on it in blind faith will invariable lead to a lot of sharp backgrounds and out-of-focus subjects!

Single & Multiple Focus Points

Any autofocus camera will give you the choice of using one or several focus points within the viewfinder. Cameras with a single focus point are simple to use because you have no choice to make. Multiple focus points greatly increase the compositional opportunities available to the wildlife photographer. The basic form is to offer points at north, south, east and west, together with a couple of focus points closer to the centre. Advanced cameras offer an ellipse of autofocus points, covering a wide area of the viewfinder and, at first glance, having a glut of options would seem the best bet. However, having lots of options means that you will probably want to change them, fiddle with them and try different options. The trouble is that by the time you have decided what to use and articulated your fingers to select the point you want, the sun will have set and everyone will be fast asleep. OK – so that may be a little exaggerated but you get the point: less is more when it comes to autofocus points and if you have a choice, choose 15 rather than 50!

Burchell's zebras drinking, Etosha National Park, Namibia

I knew that left to its own devices the autofocus would be likely to focus on the backs of the zebras, when it was vital that the heads be in sharp focus for this image to work. So, I carefully selected an autofocus point that sat right over the second zebra's head and used an aperture of f8 to bring all the other animals into sharp focus too.

◀ 35mm SLR, 500mm lens, 1/125 f8, Velvia 50

Autofocus Modes

Once you have sorted out how many autofocus points to use, the next decision is which autofocus mode to select. There are two that are common to most cameras:

▸ **One-shot** This mode locks the autofocus when the shutter button is pressed halfway and is used for subjects that are static, ie perched, sleeping or generally hanging out. If the subject moves after you have focused on it, this autofocus mode will not automatically refocus and you'll need to release and then partially depress the shutter button again to refocus.

Black-throated diver on nest, Repovesi National Park, Finland

Correct selection of the autofocus point is essential if a picture is to work. I slowly adjusted the tripod head for several minutes, positioning the lens until I had the composition I wanted and an autofocus point was squarely over the eye. It takes time but it is worth it.

▲ DSLR, 500mm lens, 1/500 f5.6, ISO 100 RAW

Golden jackal, Bandhavgarh National Park, India

Cameras with single focus points have one major problem – invariably you find yourself focusing on the centre of the frame, when in fact you might want to focus elsewhere. To get around this, most photographers focus first on their subject and then change the composition to what they really want, keeping the shutter button pressed halfway all the time to keep the autofocus locked. In this situation I was lucky that the centre autofocus point exactly matched the jackal's head; anything else would have missed the eyes and therefore the main focus of the shot.

◀ 35mm SLR, 500mm lens, 1/125 f5.6, Provia 100F

▶ **Servo/Tracking** This mode is used for anything in motion, such as a cheetah running, a flamingo flying or a crocodile lunging for its dinner! Servo focus systems constantly update the autofocus and so you have a greater chance of keeping a moving subject in focus. The trick to using it is to keep the selected autofocus point over the subject and to avoid it tracking off and focusing on the background, which it tends to do at every opportunity. If this sounds too difficult, don't worry: predictive autofocus provides a much more reliable solution.

Red-crested korhaan, Chobe National Park, Botswana

The most common mistake when using autofocus is to be lazy and always use the centre autofocus point or simply let the camera decide where to focus. Either approach can be disastrous. In this instance, if I had trusted the camera I would have had the focal point in the centre of the chest. It takes just a few seconds to select the autofocus point over your subject's eyes.

◀ 35mm SLR, 500mm lens, 1/125 f5.6, Velvia 50

Predictive Autofocus

Predictive autofocus puts the camera firmly in control of the autofocus system and allows it to predict the rate of movement of the subject. In theory, it is a magnificent way of getting superb results with even the fastest-moving subjects, because the camera can react far quicker than your eye. In reality you will need to help the camera a little:

▶ Select all of the autofocus points, not just one, to give the camera an increased chance of picking your subject and not the background.

▶ Keep the subject in the centre of the frame, where the autofocus is the most accurate.

Roebuck running, Hampshire, England

Encounters with wildlife in full flight generally happen so quickly that using servo autofocus is the only way to have any chance of getting a shot. I was out photographing rabbits (yes, I know, sad, isn't it) when this roebuck appeared on the hill above me panting heavily (silly boy had been chasing a member of the opposite sex). I managed to flick the autofocus to servo, select all the autofocus points and track his motion just as he started to run. The servo kept him in sharp focus for several seconds before I managed to cut his legs out of the frame. Here is the best of the sequence, with all limbs intact.

▲ 35mm SLR, 500mm lens, 1/250 f4, Velvia 50

Male waterbuck, Waterberg, South Africa

I had spent all afternoon with this absolutely stunning animal, and right up to this point he had won hands down by always dodging into the shadows just before I took my shot. Eventually he stood for me, albeit for 10 seconds, so I put the autofocus point right between his eyes and used one-shot autofocus. Since he was relatively still, one shot worked perfectly, whereas servo autofocus might suddenly have a mad few seconds (experienced photographers will know exactly what I mean) and refuse to focus. Having the servo autofocus needlessly tracking also drains batteries – a vital consideration when working remotely.

◀ DSLR, 500mm lens, 1/180 f5.6, ISO 100 RAW

Osprey diving, Turks and Caicos Islands

Predictive autofocus is great for birds in flight, especially against a blue sky. Since there are no distractions in the background, the autofocus is able to lock onto the subject and keep it in sharp focus.
This osprey was coming in to land at the nest and, provided I kept the bird dead centre in the viewfinder, I knew the predictive autofocus wouldn't let me down.

▲ 35mm SLR, 100-400mm lens, 1/640 f8, Sensia 200

**Mallard duck landing,
Sussex, England**

Distracting backgrounds are a nightmare when using predictive autofocus, and I've cut many slides into tiny pieces in sheer frustration at the autofocus locking onto the background rather than the subject of the picture. I tracked this mallard for several seconds before it landed, initially against the sky, and knew that as soon as it crossed the more cluttered background the autofocus would choose that instead. So, I quickly selected the central focus point and kept that right in the centre of the body, thus thwarting the tendencies of the predictive autofocus. Hah!

▲ DSLR, 300mm lens, 1/320 f5.6, ISO 100 RAW

LIGHT

There is no doubt that interesting light can make the difference between a good picture and a truly great picture. We all like to photograph in sunlight but as wildlife photographers we have to temper this with a little reality. Our subjects rarely stroll through bright sunlight and may inhabit the darkest recesses of the densest, darkest rainforest. Coupled with the likelihood that the sun won't be shining, this means that the good wildlife photographer has to be adaptable to any light conditions.

NATURAL LIGHT

There is no substitute for the wonderfully saturated sunlight just after dawn or an hour before sunset. Early and late light brings out the full colour of your subject and its fur or feathers and gives your pictures a very pleasing look. The soft light also causes fewer exposure headaches, as the latitude between extremes is far less apparent; you should still pay attention to your readings, though. An 81A filter (p24) can make the image look even more saturated for film users, while DSLR users can just add some more saturation when they process their raw files on the computer at home.

Kingfisher on perch, Oxfordshire, England

Stunning is the only word that can be used to describe the colour of kingfisher feathers in the sun, though it is one of those birds that look good at any time of the day.

◀ DSLR, 300mm lens, 1/250 f8, ISO 100 RAW

Wild dog in evening light, private game reserve, South Africa
◀ DSLR, 100-400mm lens, 1/60 f4, ISO 200 RAW, beanbag

Red lechwe, Okavango Delta, Botswana
My favourite time to shoot is first thing in the morning, when the air is clear and the light quality is wonderful. Here it picks out the coat on this lechwe perfectly, helped by an 81A warm-up filter.

▲ 35mm SLR, 600mm lens, 1/60 f5.6, Velvia 50

Barn owl outside nest, Hampshire, England

Soft evening light was vital to help correctly expose the pure white feathers of this barn owl. In this light the extremes of colour are reduced; hence you will find that the light meter will give a more accurate result. In this instance I metered on the window frame adjacent to the owl, as this was sufficiently neutral to give me a reading I could trust.

◀ 645 SLR, 300mm lens, 1/125 f4, Velvia 50

Back Lighting

The temptation with photography is always to play it safe and just take the standard shots with the sun over your shoulder falling directly onto the subject. For most photographers this achieves their goal, with a nicely balanced image that any camera can deal with and that friends, family or clients will admire. Occasionally, you will get the chance to shoot directly into the sun, either by choice or simply because that is where your subject is happily sitting (or more usually sleeping!). Shooting backlit is not something that most amateur photographers naturally consider doing, given it is not easy to achieve, but it is often a deliberate choice of professional photographers. The exact techniques for exposure of a backlit subject are essentially the same as those for a silhouette (see p78 for details). Back lighting creates images that are moody and convey a real sense of moment, and will astound anyone you show them to. The key to the backlit shot is getting the 'ring of fire' surrounding the subject. Here are a few tips to help you get those winning backlit shots:

▸ **Timing** Back lighting is only possible in the first 30 minutes after dawn and in the same period before sunset. At other times the ring of fire that surrounds your subject will be too harsh. In low light this halo effect around your subject will be red in colour and look stunning.

▸ **Backgrounds** Backlit shots work best if the background is simple, so set a low aperture of f5.6 and keep the background diffuse.

Common langur, Uttar Pradesh, India

As soon as I saw this langur in the tree I knew it had to be a backlit shot. One reason was the light on the tail; the other was the 30m drop on the other side that made a front shot impossible! So we manoeuvred the vehicle into position, I used a portrait format to keep the tail in the shot and I deliberately underexposed by –1 stop to remove the detail in the langur's body.

◀ 35mm SLR, 100-400mm lens, 1/500 f5.6, Velvia 50

Silhouettes

Following on from shooting a subject backlit is shooting a subject in silhouette. This means that the subject is completely dark – just a black shape with an outline. Silhouettes are a fantastic medium for conveying atmosphere, especially when taken against a sunset or the wonderful period just before sunrise. The technique with silhouettes is to ensure that the subject image is completely underexposed. This sounds obvious, but if you point your meter at the subject it will not be, because the camera will try to compensate for its darkness. Therefore, you need a couple of sneaky tricks:

▶ **Bright-point technique** Metering from the brightest part of the sky will cause the camera to underexpose the resulting image, which is exactly what we want. It is the same effect that happens when we look at the sun: we squint to make our field of view darker, which is exactly what the camera is doing. So choose a bright area and, if the sun is out, be careful not to point directly at it, as it could damage your camera, not to mention your eyesight.

▶ **Quick and dirty technique** Simply set your exposure compensation to –1 to –2 stops; this will completely underexpose the image.

Either way will work, and persistence will mean that you will take images that stand out from the crowd.

White rhinoceros and calf, Waterberg, South Africa

The rhino calf was causing havoc for its mother, chasing adult rhinos around and generally making itself unpopular. I waited and took this backlit shot, –1 stop underexposed. Note that both the images on this page have plenty of space around the subject. Don't crowd your backlit shots, and if you have a zoom, don't be tempted to go for the frame filler – it is a waste of a good opportunity.

▲ 35mm SLR, 300mm lens, 1/400 f5.6, Velvia 50

Southern giraffe, private game reserve, South Africa

Some animals have very recognisable profiles and these make the best candidates for a silhouette.

◀ DSLR, 300mm lens, 1/500 f8, ISO 100 RAW

Fallow deer in woodland, Sussex, England

Another tricky background. The challenge here was to get the deer in a clear patch of background without moving too much and alarming it. Once in position, I metered from the sky, darkened by an extra 1/2 stop to get a truly black deer and took the shot. Using a single autofocus point never works in these situations, as the camera struggles to find enough contrast to lock the autofocus point. Selecting all the autofocus points gives the camera a better chance of locking onto the important part of the image.

◀ 35mm SLR, 100-400mm lens, 1/500 f5.6, Sensia 100

Bottlenose dolphin, Honduras

Including the habitat in the image can give more than just a silhouette, as it creates a very atmospheric picture. Here I took the meter reading from the bright water, dialled it into manual mode and used that to shoot as the dolphin jumped. The composition was dictated by the dolphin – all I could do was to press the shutter at the right time.

◀ 35mm SLR, 17-35mm lens, 1/250 f8, Velvia 100

African elephant, private game reserve, South Africa

Sometimes it can be difficult to separate a potential silhouette from the background, even with the owner of the most recognisable ears in the world. Silhouettes only work with a clear background. To solve this I had to lie down flat on the track and try to concentrate on getting the correct exposure (using the bright-point technique; see p78), while the elephant advanced steadily towards me.

◀ 35mm SLR, 28-80mm lens, 1/250 f4, Velvia 50

PART THREE

BEING PREPARED

Probably the most crucial element of any travel and even more so for travelling wildlife photography is preparation. Wildlife is often difficult to find, let alone see or photograph, so you need to do everything you can beforehand to make your life as simple as possible in the field. Try to learn from those who have already been there and done it – there is little point in reinventing the wheel when the information you need is readily available, often at the click of a mouse.

Whooper swans at sunset, Norfolk, England
◀ DSLR, 300mm lens, 1/640 f5.6, ISO 100 RAW

PLANNING & RESEARCH

With the explosive growth in ecotourism, the travelling wildlife photographer has never had such a choice of places to go. For photographers who want to see consistently great wildlife, there are a multitude of hot spots around the world that will never disappoint. For the more adventurous there are numerous places where you can pit your wits against the local wildlife in a game of chance that may or may not yield some pictures to go home with.

No matter where you go, the key to having a great time and getting the best results is meticulous planning and thorough research. There is no point going to India to watch tigers after June, for instance, as it is simply too hot for them to be active during daylight. Tapping into local knowledge is essential and, thanks to the Internet, this is easier than ever. Luckily there are plenty of ways to ensure that you don't make a mistake and always go at the peak time for whatever it is you want to see. The following are some handy tips for your research:

▶ **Internet** Talking to other photographers via online forums is a great way of getting information, provided it is a forum you can trust. If someone is showing their pictures from a trip, they're likely to have valuable advice. Specialist travel websites such as www.lonelyplanet.com also give up-to-date, no-nonsense information about the country you will be visiting.

▶ **Travel companies** There are now many specialist travel companies that offer tours to all parts of the world. Since they want you to have a good time and come back for more, they will invariably run their tours at the peak time.

▶ **Lonely Planet** Lonely Planet guides to places around the globe from the USA to Antarctica are invaluable sources of information both before and during a trip.

Harp seal with ecotourist, Îles de la Madeleine (Magdalen Islands), Canada
Some wildlife destinations are so seasonal that only small windows exist to get the best photo-taking opportunities. These islands in Canada are such a place. For just a few weeks in March, harp seal pups crawl across ice floes, their plaintive calls the only sounds to break the intense silence. Go too early and the mothers have yet to give birth; go too late and the pups are independent enough to scuttle away from approaching humans. Timing is therefore vital and the only way to get there is to use one of the recognised tour operators.
▲ 35mm SLR, 28-80mm lens, 1/320 f5.6, Velvia 50

Black-browed albatross chick, Falkland Islands
◀ DSLR, 70-200mm lens, 1/125 f5.6, ISO 100 RAW

GOING IT ALONE

The independent travel market is accessible to most people nowadays, as the birth of low-cost airlines and booking facilities online has led to a surge in popularity of this method of travel. If you have lots of time, money and flexibility, it is possible to travel independently to photograph wildlife. Most professional photographers choose to travel in this manner purely for the flexibility of doing so, and certainly not because they are rich. However, a great many of the wildlife wonders of the world are found in locations that are reasonably difficult to access and may be potentially dangerous for the unwary traveller. Furthermore, for its own sake much wildlife is highly protected and therefore tourist access is restricted. For instance, visits to the Galápagos Islands or to Antarctica are strictly controlled and only possible with recognised tour operators – canoeing is definitely not an option! Seriously, unless you do have bags of time, the best option for the travelling wildlife photographer is to join some form of organised tour, preferably one with a photography slant since this is the main aim of your visit.

THE ORGANISED TOUR

The trick with an organised tour is to go on one that specialises in the activity that you are most interested in. Photographic tours generally maximise their time in the field and will put you in the right location during the best light – right about the time when more generalist sightseeing tours will be having sundowners at the bar. It is a good idea to travel with like-minded people when attempting wildlife photography. Wildlife photography often means early mornings and late evenings, which may not be terribly appealing to a group of travellers without this main focus. Try to find a tour that has only a small number of participants or, better still, get the tour company to organise a bespoke tour just for you and your companions. This will work out to be marginally more expensive but, in terms of flexibility and your photographic results, it will be leaps and bounds ahead of other tours.

AFRICAN SAFARIS

Perhaps the most common adventure for the modern traveller in search of wildlife subjects to photograph is an African safari. Whether you are staying in a five-star lodge or camping out under the stars, Africa is a place that hooks you and never lets you go. Africa offers a fantastic diversity of wildlife, too, from the game-rich plains of Kenya to the wild and desolate Namib Desert, and many travellers return time after time to sample different areas.

The subject of safari is so vast that a book could easily be written on the subject. Perhaps the most difficult aspect of a safari is choosing where to go in the first place. For first timers the obvious choice is East Africa, with its easily accessible parks and incredible concentrations of wildlife. For the more adventurous, southern Africa holds many jewels such as the Okavango Delta, the Skeleton Coast of Namibia and the Sabi Sands Game Reserve of South Africa. Whichever destination you choose, it pays to book via a recognised operator and leave nothing to chance upon your arrival. Specialised photographic tours offer the best option in terms of being in the field for the maximum amount of time and will provide a great insight into what Africa has to offer. An African safari is a wonderful experience and should not be missed – your memories of the sights and sounds will last a lifetime.

Leopard and tourist vehicle, MalaMala Game Reserve, South Africa

For years I had wanted to go to MalaMala to photograph the leopards. Everyone I spoke to recommended it and every book I read had amazing pictures by other photographers. When I finally got there I was expecting a lot... and it delivered, with seven leopard sightings in seven days. It was an expensive trip but worth every penny.

▲ DSLR, 70-200mm lens, 1/500 f5.6, ISO 100 RAW

WILDLIFE HOT SPOTS

Every country of the world has its wildlife hot spots. These are places where gatherings of wildlife make it easy for those who are constrained by time. Here is a list of the some of the more popular locations, but it is by no means exhaustive.

The Everglades, USA

These world-famous wetlands at the southern tip of Florida provide a superb habitat for diverse wildlife. Particularly good for birds such as the roseate spoonbill, osprey, all manner of water birds and the ever-present alligators, the Everglades are one of the prime wildlife viewing areas in the USA. There is good access throughout, with a road system backed up by experienced boat operators, and a huge selection of accommodation options, from top-notch digs to budget-priced hotels. The Everglades are superb for everyone and ideal for the independent traveller. Also close to one of the most popular tourist destinations in the States, this region is handy for combining your wildlife photography interests with those of the rest of the family. The best times to visit are January and February.

Antarctica

The ultimate wildlife-cruising destination, the vast continent of Antarctica is home to the penguin family. These wonderful birds, ranging from the magnificent emperors and kings to the ever-friendly rockhopper, will never fail to offer you superb photographic opportunities. Antarctica is not just the realm of the penguin either; it is home to a wide

Roseate spoonbill preening its feathers, the Everglades, USA

This beautiful shot was taken late one evening from a road that runs alongside one of the many lakes. That is the beauty of the Everglades – great access to wildlife. Accommodation for all tastes is available, but given the local insect life and certain reptiles that have far too many teeth, personally I would avoid camping.

◀ 35mm SLR, 300mm lens, 1/125 f5.6, Velvia 50

Gentoo penguin landing on beach, Falkland Islands
Any Antarctic cruise worthy of the name will stop at several of the sub-Antarctic islands before reaching the continent itself. These islands are real wildlife havens and really fragile environments where damage can last a lifetime, so please treat the wildlife and the environment with care and respect. Do that and Antarctica will reward you every single day you are close to her shores.
▲ DSLR, 300mm lens, 1/1000 f4, ISO 100 RAW

variety of bird and marine life. It is reasonably easy to get to, with many tour operators offering cruises to the main hot spots, although some will not be ideal for the travelling wildlife photographer. Try to pick a photographic cruise with around 100 passengers, as this will maximise your landing time as well as presenting less pressure to the fragile eco-systems you are visiting. Antarctica is a long way from anywhere and getting there takes a major effort, so don't expect to do this trip on a budget. And though it is expensive, it is definitely a bargain in terms of the experience you will have. The best time to visit is from late November to February.

Alaska, USA
One of the last wilderness areas on earth, Alaska is home to such wildlife icons as the wolf, grizzly bear, bald eagle and moose. Local hot spots such as Denali National Park, Brooks Falls and Haines offer fantastic wildlife viewing of these magnificent animals but you'll need a good local guide. Alaska provides a real diversity of wildlife too, with some of the best whale-watching in the world at Glacier Bay and rivers that turn pink with migrating salmon during the late summer. Alaska is truly awe-inspiring. The best time to visit de-pends on what you want to see, because Alaska is a year-round destination. In general, the peak wildlife viewing is from June to September.

Churchill, Canada
Every year hundreds of polar bears gather at the tip of Cape Churchill to await the forma-tion of ice that will take them to their feeding grounds in Hudson Bay. This has made the town of Churchill the self-proclaimed polar bear–watching capital of the world and

Polar bear and tourist van, Churchill, Canada

Churchill is the one place in the world where you can get as close as this to polar bears in the safety of a vehicle.

◀ 35mm SLR, 70-200mm lens, 1/60 f5.6, Velvia 50

nowhere else can you get so close in complete safety to these magnificent animals. Custom-built vehicles called tundra buggies ferry tourists out to see the bears; these vehicles are warm and comfortable and provide great platforms for photography. Churchill is not well suited to the independent traveller, as the tundra buggies are privately owned. Places are booked up fast by tour operators, so book early. It is a great destination at other times of the year, too: in February the northern lights are spectacular, and in the summer months beluga whales migrate into the Churchill River. If you want to see polar bears, the best times to visit are October and November.

The Okavango Delta, Botswana

A mixture of swamp, wetlands and savanna habitats, southern Africa's Okavango Delta is a wildlife photographer's jewel. It is superb for bird life and big mammals, with all the usual predators in abundance. The delta offers many accommodation options, too, from rough bush camping to five-star lodges complete with chandeliers. The great attraction

Cheetah, Masai Mara National Reserve, Kenya
Perhaps the best reason for visiting the Masai Mara is the chance to spend time with its resident population of cheetahs. Time is the key with cheetahs – spend as much of it with them as you can and maybe, just maybe, you'll be rewarded with the sight of the fastest mammal on earth speeding across the plains. It is a sight you will never forget.
▲ DSLR, 500mm lens, 1/180 f8, ISO 100 RAW

is the lack of other people. You will rarely see more than two or three other vehicles on safari, which gives you a true sense of Africa and an unforgettable safari experience. The best time to visit is from August to December.

Masai Mara National Reserve, Kenya
In complete contrast to the Okavango Delta, Kenya's Masai Mara National Reserve is always jam packed with tourists and vehicles. Don't let this put you off, however, as the game viewing and photographic opportunities here are probably the best in Africa. Every year the annual wildebeest migration passes through the Mara along with its accompanying predators. Lodges are of a good standard, there are some (albeit limited) options for camping and the Mara is only an hour's flight from the international airport in Nairobi. Although tourism in the Masai Mara is strictly governed to protect the environment, it's best to make sure that your safari company has good environmental credentials, as it is also up to travellers to act responsibly (see p113). The best time to visit is from January to March and from July to October.

The Pantanal, Brazil
One of the greatest wetland areas in the world, the Pantanal is great for the wildlife photographer who is after something a little more challenging. Bird life is superb, featuring rarities such as the hyacinth macaw. Jaguars patrol the forests and mammals such as anteaters and tapirs walk the plains. Lodges are plentiful and most charge reasonable rates.

Toco toucan, the Pantanal, Brazil

The attraction of the Pantanal is that the wildlife is totally different from the more commonly seen African wildlife. This toucan sat obligingly above our vehicle for several minutes while we tried to edge one way and then another to get a clear shot. Previously my only experience with toucans was from watching the Guinness advertisements; seeing them in the wild was so special and an illustration of what the Pantanal has to offer.

▲ 35mm SLR, 300mm lens, 1/320 f5.6, Velvia 50

In fact the only real difficulty is getting there, as it is in a remote location, but this is also one of the reasons it is so pristine. The best time to visit is from August to October.

Galápagos Islands & Costa Rica

Fantastic for bird life in particular, Costa Rica is a lush, tropical location and often serves as a stopping-off point for a visit to the Galápagos Islands (Ecuador). One of the most famous and visited ecotourism destinations in the world, the Galápagos Islands are also some of the most strictly protected. All access is from licensed tourist boats and landings are strictly controlled. The native wildlife is incredibly friendly and the islands are perhaps best known for their giant tortoises and the antics of brightly coloured boobies. Lonely Planet's *Watching Wildlife: Galápagos Islands* provides listings for all the main sites and is a must-have for anyone serious about visiting the islands. The best time to visit is from January to April, as this is the breeding season for many animals; however, from June to November is the best time for sea birds.

Madagascar

Madagascar is a unique location with wildlife you won't find anywhere else in the world. Lemurs, of course, are high on the wish lists of most photographers visiting this wonderful island but there are plenty of other creatures to photograph here, including chameleons, fossas, birds, creepy crawlies galore and incredible native plant life. Much of the wildlife is restricted to protected areas, because the rainforests are under considerable threat from logging and development, but this makes the animals simple to locate. Your tourist money will also go a long way towards saving the wildlife and boosting the local economy. The best time to visit is from September to October.

GETTING THERE

At some stage you will take your gear abroad, perhaps on a group photographic holiday or alone. Either way, you'll be joining the international stress club of travelling wildlife photographers and need to take precautions to ensure that you and your gear stay together.

Airline Allowances

Airlines are very strict on their baggage allowances (check beforehand if in doubt), typically allowing one piece of luggage in the cabin weighing no more than 7kg to 8kg plus checked baggage weighing a total of 20kg. In reality, they may bend these rules a little, but increasingly they're weighing hand baggage too. Checked baggage will usually be accepted if it's a few kilograms over the limit or you will simply have to accept excess-baggage payments (or pack more lightly in the first place). Most airlines offer an excess baggage rate that is cheaper if purchased ahead of time rather than at the airport. These limits are likely to become more strictly enforced in future. Laptop bags are also accepted as an extra piece of cabin baggage provided they are not too bulky. These limits are not negotiable at check-in time. Under no circumstances get angry – airline staff are only doing their jobs!

To be honest, most of the hassle of travelling by air comes from lugging 500–600mm lenses around, which will not be an issue for most photographers. Two camera bodies, two or three zoom or fixed lenses and other assorted junk can easily be transported in your rucksack as normal cabin baggage. The choice of rucksack too can be crucial; brands such as Crumpler make excellent photo rucksacks that look like everyday backpacks.

Masai giraffe feeding, Masai Mara National Reserve, Kenya
Travelling with the minimum amount of gear you need is the best way to ensure you get the maximum from your days out in the field. Good research should tell you how close you can get to animals in the area, and this, to some extent, will dictate what you take with you. For example, when I go to the Masai Mara I find myself using my 70-200mm and 300mm lenses more than anything else as the wildlife is so tolerant of vehicles.
▲ DSLR, 70-200mm lens, 1/320 f5.6, ISO 100 RAW

Packing

Cabin Baggage

Packing for travel is an art form, and packing with camera gear is for the grandmasters of this. Packing your cabin baggage is likely to create the most stress but can be reduced by adopting the right attitude from the start. The philosophy is to take the absolute minimum you need to shoot, in case your checked baggage fails to make it or is routed elsewhere (it does happen). Items that fall into this category are your camera body; your longest and widest-angle lenses; a spare battery, complete with charger and cable; a portable downloader with its charger; all your memory cards; and an empty beanbag. With the rest of your kit, you can transport it safely in your checked baggage – keep your fingers crossed that it makes it to the other end when you do.

Film users note that it is essential that you take your film on board with you, as checked baggage is subject to *very* strong X-rays that will fog your film. Of course, your film will have to pass through the standard airport X-rays, but these have been proved to be perfectly safe for all film of ISO 400 and below. Tests have shown that only repeated and prolonged exposures to X-rays of film above ISO 400 can cause slight fogging. If you are concerned, put your film in a clear plastic bag and politely ask for a hand search. If the security staff

refuse, then put your film in a tray and let it pass through the X-ray machine – it will be perfectly fine. Do not under any circumstances use lead-lined bags, as they will mask the X-ray, which will either result in your baggage being intensively searched or, worse still, a more probing exploration.

Checked Baggage

Again, only take what you will really need and double up on anything vital. Ask yourself some simple questions: do I need my tripod? (If you're working from a vehicle, you don't.) Do I need both my 100-400mm and 70-200 zoom lenses? Either will probably suffice. Batteries are a major concern at all times so it pays to take too many rather than too few, whether they are AAs or rechargeable NiMh packs. Doubling up is important for stuff that you will be unlikely to obtain locally, such as a charger and USB cables – they weigh little but are irreplaceable.

Use socks or clothes to pack around your camera gear and, for extra protection, pack fragile stuff inside boots or shoes. Luggage will be roughly treated regardless of the number of fragile stickers you place on your bags, so err on the side of caution and do all you can to prevent breakages. Wrap tripods in fleeces, outdoor coats and trousers, protect

the tripod head with some thick socks and, ideally, put it inside its own padded bag. Lots of small bundles of tightly wrapped gear then need to be packed into a hard-shell bag; packing these bundles as tightly as possible will protect the equipment and help to keep it safe. When packing photographic gear there is no point in being concerned about creasing your clothes. Your camera equipment takes priority – wildlife photography is not a fashion parade.

The golden rule when packing checked baggage is to make it anonymous. Checking in a camera rucksack or camera bag will alert the eagle eyes of would-be thieves to potentially rich pickings. It's fine to transport everything in the camera bag, but you might want to place it in a nondescript outer bag. Using an external padlock and or cable ties is also useful to keep your bag secure from prying hands, but you must be prepared to open the bag for officials if required. US entry requirements now dictate that all checked baggage will be searched and all locks will be cut, so choose a bag that can be easily closed by customs after inspection, such as a large sports bag. Suitcases may be useful, but if you're travelling independently they can be awkward and inflexible for further travel once you reach your destination.

Grizzly bear, Alaska, USA
I adopt the policy that whenever I travel, especially when camping in remote locations such as Alaska to photograph grizzly bears, I have to have the minimum kit – longest lens, zoom lens, one camera body, one battery, one charger plus cables, one downloader, all film or memory cards, an empty beanbag and a cleaning kit – in my cabin baggage that will allow me to shoot at the other end, just in case the rest of my gear doesn't make it. A spare pair of underwear is always handy, too!

◀ DSLR, 500mm lens, 1/60 f5.6, ISO 200 RAW

AT YOUR DESTINATION

WORKING IN THE FIELD

Once you get to your destination the fun can really begin, and you can put your grounding in basic camera craft into practice. Here are some essential facts you need to know while working in the field.

On Arrival

When you arrive at your destination, get everything unpacked and check that all of your equipment has arrived safely. If you have access to power, recharge your camera batteries and anything else that works on rechargeables. Set up an area with all of your chargers all hooked up and ready; after a long day in the field the last thing you want is to fiddle around with endless cables. Keeping these all in one place should help you to remember to unplug and pack them when you come to leave (not to mention making it easier to find things when returning after dark).

Mandarin duck, Sussex, England

I don't care whether I am photographing a lesser spotted whatever or a blue pied reticulated something – I just love being out in the field with wildlife. I'm never in a rush, always patient and generally have a smile on my face. This image shows a beautiful mandarin duck that I spent a total of four hours with, as he strutted his stuff trying to attract the attention of a female. It was beautiful to watch and less than two miles from my home – proof that you don't have to travel miles to see great wildlife.

▲ DSLR, 500mm lens, 1/320 f5.6, ISO 100 RAW

Grizzly bear in habitat, Alaska, USA

◀ DSLR, 70-200mm lens, 1/60 f11, ISO 200 RAW

Cleaning Your Equipment

The next task, and this should become a daily routine (or a bit of a chore depending on your point of view), is to clean your gear. Look at any professional's gear and it will be scrupulously clean. Dust, particularly when travelling, is the major enemy of the photographer. This applies particularly to those using digital equipment and it pays to clean everything whenever you get the chance.

Film Camera

▸ Without a film loaded, open the back, hold it upside down and use an air blower to blow any dust or hairs from the film plane.
▸ Take the lens off, hold the camera upside down and use the air blower to clean the mirror. This is not really essential as anything on the mirror will not appear on the film, but a mucky viewfinder is distracting.

African leopard, MalaMala Game Reserve, South Africa

We can learn a lot from the animal kingdom, and keeping our vital equipment clean is something that we have in common. We found this lovely female relaxing on a termite mound and she groomed herself for at least 20 minutes, getting everything shipshape. Rather than disturbing her by blasting away with the motor drive, I timed each shot to get the tongue out at the end of the paw and used a small amount of flash to fill in the shadows.

◀ DSLR, 70-200mm lens with 1.4x teleconverter, 1/320 f5.6, ISO 100 RAW, flash

Burchell's zebra stallions fighting, Masai Mara National Reserve, Kenya

Being prepared is the name of the game, as moments like this occur suddenly and are over in seconds. Luckily my camera was set up and ready to shoot, with the aperture at f5.6 (which by default selects a fast shutter speed) and all three million focus points selected.

◀ DSLR, 300mm lens, 1/500 f8, ISO 100 RAW

European brown bear, eastern Finland

The beauty of a DSLR is that you can change the ISO for every shot – surprisingly, many photographers forget this. Start off with ISO 100 as that will give the highest-quality results, then move to ISO 200 (little difference in reality from ISO 100) as the light levels fall. In low-light conditions, or on dull days, do not be afraid to raise your ISO to 400, as it is better to get a sharp image at ISO 400 than a blurry one at ISO 200. Unless you want to create 'art' (a polite term for unintentional blur, under- or overexposure, or just getting it wrong), avoid using higher ISO values; if you are shooting for black and white images, ignore this and shoot at ISO 800 or ISO 1600 for a lovely grainy effect. As the light levels dropped in the forest, I changed my ISO from 100 to 200 and then finally to 400, which allowed me to continue shooting even in the lowest light.

▲ DSLR, 70-200mm lens with 1.4x teleconverter, 1/60 f4, ISO 400 RAW

DSLR

▸ Only use a natural air blower (such as a Giotto RocketAir) to clean a DSLR sensor; never use a compressed air blower, as it can blow moisture droplets onto the sensor. Never clean the sensor with a swab: one slip will result in a useless camera and a very expensive replacement (sensors cannot be repaired).

▸ Only clean the DSLR in a closed environment, such as a room or tent, where more dust cannot get onto the sensor.

▸ Take the lens off, choose the 'Clean Sensor' option from the menu and press the shutter to open the mirror. Hold the DSLR with the lens mount facing the floor so that any dust will fall out. Use the air blower a few times, taking care not to touch the sensor and quickly inspect the sensor to check for any hairs, foreign bodies etc that may have worked their way inside.

▸ Turn the DSLR off to reset the mirror, put on a lens and take a shot with the picture well out of focus (using the manual focus ring).

▸ Check the LCD image for signs of any hairs or large foreign bodies. It is amazing what can get stuck inside.

▸ Avoid cleaning the sensor excessively – once a day will be perfectly adequate. When in the field, change lenses as little as possible to minimise the chance of dust getting to the sensor (another good reason to use a long-range zoom). Remember: prevention is better than cure.

Shooting in the Field – Basic Camera Setup

Before you travel it is essential to practise using your camera and understand all the basics of exposure, composition and autofocus prior to attempting it in the field. Familiarity in this instance should breed successful images and will be vital in the heat of the moment. Wildlife encounters can be very short and you'll often be shooting on instinct and pure adrenaline, so anything that improves your chances of getting it spot on will help. To ensure you don't make a horrendous mistake and go home with nothing to be proud of, here is a simple checklist:

▸ **Media** Always load a new film or have a fresh memory card for the start of each photography session or outing. Having just a few shots left will have you come unstuck at some stage in your journey.

▸ **Power** Always have the camera switched on and ready to shoot. This is important as some DSLRs take several seconds to power up and it will use up less battery power than if you constantly turn it on and off.

▸ **Exposure** Set the camera to aperture priority (AV) and to f5.6. This will guarantee a decent shutter speed, which will probably be more important than a huge depth of field if you come across a picture unexpectedly. You can change your shooting parameters as you work (and if the subject stays around long enough to allow you to).

▸ **Autofocus** Set the autofocus to one shot and select all available focus points. This will allow you to shoot quickly and accurately; then if you have time you can select an individual focus point or experiment further.

▸ **Protection** If it is dusty, keep the camera and lens covered with a towel, pillowcase or coat, especially if you are in a vehicle. In a wet climate, a waterproof cover like an Aquatech will be a great investment.

Little egret fishing, Yala National Park, Sri Lanka

A DSLR can only shoot a finite number of images before it locks you out to write them to the memory card. It's a sure bet this will happen at the most inconvenient moment; one advantage JPEG has over RAW is that it takes longer to reach lockout. Lockout will occur whether you shoot JPEG or RAW and will doubtless cause much frustration and fruitless pressing of the shutter button. The best approach is to keep this in mind, as you would if you were nearing the end of your film. Pick your images carefully, only take good images and resist shooting just anything that moves. You can then spend less time poring over images when you get home.

▲ DSLR, 300mm lens, 1/1000 f4, ISO 200 RAW

Black-browed albatross, Falkland Islands

DSLR sensors are very prone to overexposing any white feathers, so make sure your LCD histogram is slightly to the left of centre so that it slightly underexposes these subjects (p54). This will ensure that the beautiful detail in the feathers is recorded perfectly for all to see and enjoy.

▲ DSLR, 300mm lens, 1/1000 f5.6, ISO 100 RAW

WORKING OFF THE BEATEN TRACK

Most photographers at some time or another will work away from the loving embrace of a power socket. With a little forethought and careful technique, you can work comfortably in such environments and enjoy them without forever getting stressed about power, or the lack of it.

Power Considerations

Most consumer-film SLRs use off-the-shelf batteries and so power is not an issue, provided you take plenty with you. For those with rechargeable power packs or anyone with a DSLR, energy is a real issue, as these power sources are very energy hungry. If you're on a day trip, power is not likely to be a problem, since you're able to take a few spare batteries along. A lot of places where you may stay overseas (lodges, boats etc) supply power via a generator, which is no problem so long as you acknowledge their limitations. Often the power will be switched on for a restricted period during the day, so it's advisable to charge your batteries at every opportunity, whether they need it or not. If in doubt, charge it! Since generators create a voltage spike when they are first switched on, it is also prudent to have a circuit-breaking RCD (residual current device) plug between the generator outlet and your chargers, as damage can occur easily. It is important that you research the power situation thoroughly before you travel; turning up and hoping for the best is generally not a clever idea. Don't forget that in some areas where they are reliant on a generator, other things will have priority over your equipment – be considerate of the needs of others.

Female mandarin duck taking off, Sussex, England
Most good wildlife photographs involve a lot of waiting and few brief moments of action. This waiting time should be used productively to set up the exposure so it is one less thing to think about. Use the LCD histogram to fine-tune the exposure, then put it into manual mode and forget about it unless the light changes drastically. Then, when moments of high action occur, such as this mandarin duck erupting from the water, you'll be ready to nail the shot.

▲ DSLR, 300mm lens, 1/1000 f4, ISO 200 RAW

Desert black rhino, Namib Desert, Namibia
Camping in the middle of the Namibian desert for two weeks chasing after images of desert black rhinos, we had no power at all. One option was to take along a small generator, but the noise would have spoiled the experience; a great solution is to use a vehicle (bad luck if you're on a camel) to create the power via a device called an inverter. These units either plug into the vehicle's cigarette-lighter socket or have a connection directly to the car battery. The best ones are small and light and can be used to power all manner of devices.
▲ DSLR, 500mm lens, 1/250 f8, ISO 200 RAW

Conserving Energy
As with anything that has a finite supply, being economical is essential. Learn to use your camera efficiently; it can mean the difference between getting those winning shots and cursing a dead camera when you want it most. How you use your camera in the field can have a huge effect on the amount of energy it uses.

Rufescent tiger-heron, the Pantanal, Brazil
One of the great advantages of film cameras is that most can use off-the-shelf batteries at a push. Taking this image in the Pantanal, where I was without power for a week with no method of recharging, presented little problem as I had an AA battery pack.
◀ 35mm SLR, 600mm lens, 1/125 f5.6, Velvia 50

Johnny rook, Falkland Islands

Staying in a hut on the Falkland Islands, we had only a small solar panel to recharge our batteries. Charging from wind or solar power presents no problem provided you realise that it will probably take a lot longer to recharge your batteries and the charge may not last as long.

◀ DSLR, 300mm lens, 1/500 f8, ISO 100 RAW

Image-Stabilised Lenses

These lenses derive all of their power from your camera battery. In general, the bigger the lens, the greater the amount of power it will drain from your battery. Continually pressing the shutter button to engage the autofocus and stabiliser function when you have little intention of taking a shot will drain your batteries quickly. Use your binoculars to watch wildlife – they take no power at all.

DSLR LCD & Chimping

The quickest way to drain your batteries in a DSLR is the continual use of the LCD screen. This can be drastically reduced by turning off the option to display the image or histogram every time a shot is taken. Practise at home first so you don't need to keep referring to the histogram when it really matters.

Resist continuously reviewing your images on the LCD. Protagonists of 'chimping' state that they are checking if they have got the shot, which is flawed for the following reasons: you cannot judge anything about the shot from the LCD screen apart from exposure (using the histogram); it is too late to do anything about the composition; and, finally, by 'chimping' you are missing the action that is happening in front of you. By all means check the LCD for exposure, but you only need to do so very occasionally – it's your skill that matters.

Downloaders

On a long trip, a portable downloader is as vital as the DSLR itself, as it stores all of your hard-earned images. All downloaders have notoriously short-life batteries, so keep them fully charged at all times and take spare batteries with you if possible. The most sophisticated downloaders have LCD screens that, again, can really drain the batteries if used excessively, so only use them in the field for downloading and not for viewing your images.

WORKING FROM HIDES

Most wildlife that you encounter will be sufficiently familiar with vehicles or the sight of humans on foot to allow you to get reasonably close for a picture. However, there are some species that are just too shy or too smart to tolerate any human presence. For these situations the only option is to use a hide to provide protection from prying eyes and to mask human scent from sensitive noses. Permanent hides are usually built where wildlife tends to congregate regularly, such as at water holes or feeding sites; temporary hides are erected for seasonal opportunities, such as nest photography.

Golden eagle with captured rabbit, Kuusamo, Finland
I photographed this golden eagle from a permanent wooden hide. The main problem was that there was no room for a tripod, so I had to use a beanbag for one lens and a tripod head on a purpose-built clamp for the other. Two important points are to keep the end of the lens from sticking out too far from the hide and to make sure that it is camouflaged to some degree. Although permanent hides do mask movement inside very well, try to keep all movements and chatter to a minimum.
▲ DSLR, 300mm lens with 1.4x teleconverter, 1/60 f4, ISO 400 RAW

Roebuck, Hampshire, England
For such a shy animal as this, a temporary hide needs to be used. There are many designs available, all of which are really glorified tents with big windows for lenses. The best hides come with a built-in floor, which is very useful for keeping snakes from using the hide as a warm place to sleep. The cardinal sins when using a temporary hide are to let your subject see you entering or leaving it and to hit the sides when your subject is looking straight at you.
◀ DSLR, 500mm lens, 1/500 f5.6, ISO 100 RAW

Red-throated diver on lake, Repovesi National Park, Finland

Some birds are so intolerant of human presence that to get close to them requires extended periods in the hide. To photograph this red-throated diver I spent a total of 20 hours in the hide each day, only leaving under the cover of darkness to answer the call of nature.

▲ DSLR, 500mm lens, 1/250 f5.6, ISO 100 RAW

Crested caracara, the Pantanal, Brazil

By far the best nonpermanent hide is your own car, as most species will readily accept it; use either a beanbag or a specially designed door or window clamp to support your lens. Putting a cloth up against the passenger window will also help mask your silhouette, which could give you a few extra seconds for your photography. I saw this caracara well ahead of me on the road and killed the engine so that I idled up to it quietly.

◀ 35mm SLR, 300mm lens with 1.4x teleconverter, 1/320 f5.6, Velvia 50

WORKING IN EXTREME CLIMATES

Much of the world's wildlife lives in remote areas that are prone to climatic extremes. Unfortunately, camera gear and extreme climates are not a good mix and you will have to take precautions to protect your valuable kit from the ravages of mother earth.

Cold Climates

The biggest enemy here is the cold's effect of draining batteries. Most battery packs are designed to work at room temperature and above. If you are working in temperatures below zero, your batteries will last considerably less time than you would expect and you need to take measures to make sure you have enough power to shoot. The key to retaining power is to keep the batteries warm. One approach is to surround spare batteries with chemical warming packs buried deep inside your clothing so that they also gain heat from your body. When your camera battery finally freezes, swap it over with the warm one from inside your clothing. The best solution is to have an external battery pack buried in your clothing with the warming packs surrounding it; a cable can then connect it to the camera. At low temperatures film is very susceptible to snapping, so it is best to always keep it safely tucked away until it is needed.

Stellar sea eagle, Hokkaido, Japan

All of us have images or memories that come to mind when we look at our pictures. For this image mine is simply that I was so cold I thought my hands were going to fall off. It was –28°C (–18°F), with a wind-chill on top, and my batteries were freezing up every few minutes.

◀ 35mm SLR, 600mm lens, 1/1250 f4, Velvia 50

Highland cattle, the Grampians, Scotland
Heavy snowfalls are a real bonus for the photographer, transforming a mediocre scene into something more memorable. When I saw this cow in a field next to the road I knew that it would be a good image, because the snow-covered trees behind added something extra to the shot. Metering was difficult so I chose my tightest spot-meter pattern and used the centre of the nose, which at least gave me a decent reading.

▲ 35mm SLR, 28-80mm lens, 1/60 f4, Provia 100F

Mountain lion, California, USA
Sometimes you will be lucky enough to photograph in a snowstorm and there is a right way and a wrong way to do it. The right way is to use a very fast shutter speed to freeze (no pun intended) the motion of the snow so that it is easy to see in the final shot; blurring it with a slow shutter speed generally ends up as a mess.

◄ 35mm SLR, 70-200mm lens, 1/250 f4, Provia 100F

Greater spotted woodpecker, Oxfordshire, England
There has been a lot written about the performance of DSLRs and memory cards in cold climates. Unless you are working at extremes of –29°C (–20°F) or less, you have no need to worry; if you are working in these temperatures then a warming cover may have to be used to keep the sensor at a working temperature.

◀ DSLR, 300mm lens, 1/250 f5.6, ISO 200 RAW

Possibly the most common mistake made in cold climates is to bring your cameras and lenses from the cold into a warm environment. This will cause immediate condensation inside and outside the lens, sometimes with catastrophic results. The best solution is to put your gear into a rucksack or bag before you come in from the cold and store it in a location where the temperature difference between inside and outside is minimal. Make sure that you have removed the batteries and memory cards before you take the bag inside, as you will need to recharge and download them in the warm and should not open the bag once indoors. If you absolutely have to bring the bag into a warm environment, keep it sealed for several hours before opening it; this will allow the gear to warm up very slowly to room temperature and avoid condensation from developing.

Hot, Dusty Climates
Heat and dust can cause problems for both the film and digital photographer. The main enemy is dust and the DSLR sensor is seriously affected by this demon. To prevent dust from getting into the sensor, simply minimise the number of times you expose the internal

African leopard, private game reserve, South Africa

The heat of the African sun cannot be underestimated and keeping your gear out of the sun is important in order to prevent internal damage from ruining your trip. It is easy to forget that you have left the camera exposed on the roof of the vehicle, so make sure when you are not shooting that you bring it back into a shady spot or cover it well. Take a tip from the animals and spend the hottest part of the day in the shade.

◀ DSLR, 300mm lens with 1.4x teleconverter, 1/500 f5.6, ISO 100 RAW

Desert elephant dust bathing, Hoanib River, Namibia

Dusty and sandy environments are dangerous for cameras of all kinds and you need to take great care of your equipment in these locations. Minimise the chances of getting particles inside the camera by keeping it covered as much as possible and try to avoid changing the lens and opening up the camera as much as possible. This image of a desert elephant was taken from the dried-out riverbed. I brought the camera out from its blanket cover only when absolutely needed and returned it immediately afterwards.

◀ DSLR, 300mm lens, 1/250 f5.6, ISO 200 RAW

workings of the camera to the atmosphere by not changing lenses too often. If you do have to change the lens, make sure that it is not while you're exposed to a thick dust cloud or moving along in a car. Dust on the lens is not a major issue, but it pays to have your camera and lens wrapped in a towel, pillowcase or coat to protect it from the worst.

Heat can really damage film if the back of the camera is left exposed to direct sunlight for a prolonged period of time. A few hours in 32°C (90°F) heat will do the trick if you want to ruin your film. The same is true for the DSLR, as the hotter the sensor becomes, the greater the likelihood of damage. A lesser concern is that a hot sensor introduces more signal noise into your digital file and hence affects the quality of your images. To avoid these issues, keep your cameras in the shade when they are not required and cover them when they are.

Wet Climates

Camera electronics and water do not mix at all and it is essential that you take precautions against the destructive effects of rain or salt water. A simple solution is to place a plastic bag over the camera and create a small hole in it for the eye-cup; this is useful against the harmful effects of sea spray but is useless for any significant amounts of rain. For these situations you will need a waterproof cover that is made for the job. These vary from the very cheap to all-in-one totally waterproof covers (such as those produced by Aquatech) for the camera and lens; while the latter are expensive, they allow you to continue taking pictures in all kinds of weather and protect your valuable photographic investment.

Cheetah cubs playing, Masai Mara National Reserve, Kenya
Rain is a fantastic medium to photograph in and you should always try to stay out as long as you can in a storm. Use the same technique as with snow: shoot with a high shutter speed to freeze the individual drops of water as they fall. Rain also encourages playtime in some animals. We had sat through an hour's deluge with a family of cheetahs sheltering under our vehicle; as soon as the rain eased off, however, the three cubs started to play and chase each other around. Although the light was very challenging, I like this shot as the trails of water from the tails add to the fun of the moment.
▲ DSLR, 500mm lens, 1/250 f4, ISO 200 RAW

CLOTHING

As well as the camera equipment, it is vitally important that you look after yourself when out and about taking pictures. Having the right clothes for the job can make a huge difference. The old adage that 'there is no bad weather, just bad clothing' has more than a ring of truth to it. A comfortable photographer is a relaxed one and being relaxed can only lead to positive results in your photography.

Cold Weather

Wear layers of clothing, starting with a thin base layer against your skin and working up towards an outer waterproof layer. Down-filled jackets are superb for extremely cold climates and perhaps offer the greatest warmth of any clothing. They are also notoriously impractical in slightly warmer climates or in the wet. In those cases, a layered system, such as the Páramo directional clothing range, is always better as it gives you the greatest flexibility in a changeable climate. In cold climates most heat loss is from the head, so it is vital to wear a warm, breathable hat. Extremities are also at risk: a pair of thin, silk gloves against your skin and then much thicker gloves over the top provides a good layering system for your hands, and a similar principle should be applied to footwear. Make sure that your boots are not too tight to allow a layer of insulating air between your socks and the boot walls.

Hot Weather

Breathable clothing is the best option for hot climates, particularly the type that draws the moisture away from your body to keep you cool. This applies equally to trousers – the best are those that allow venting at the sides to let out excess heat. Also, try to get clothing that has a decent SPF sun-protection rating and ensure that you are covered up at all times and protected with a high-factor sun block. A good wide-brimmed sunhat is a must too. Make sure that you have a means of securing it to your head if it becomes windy; you will not please an elephant one bit if you lose your hat in front of it – in fact, it could spark a stampede! Also try to pick subtle, muted colours such as greens and browns, or light, neutral beiges; bright colours will do little for you when you're trying to get close to wildlife (even in a vehicle).

Oystercatcher on nest, Lancashire, England

Birds at the nest need to be given tremendous respect, as some species will abandon their eggs if disturbed. When photographing this oystercatcher, I did so with my longest lens and from a car, as I knew this would not cause the bird any stress and would not advertise her nest to predators.

◀ DSLR, 500mm lens with 1.4x teleconverter, 1/500 f5.6, ISO 100 RAW

PHOTO ETIQUETTE

Wildlife photographers are privileged to see the natural world and share it with others via their photographs. Equally important to taking these photographs is doing it in a responsible and ethical manner.

Respect for Wildlife

As a travelling wildlife photographer you are an ambassador for other photographers and should consider yourself a guest of the animal kingdom. One bad encounter with a human could turn a friendly animal into a shy or potentially dangerous one, and with a youngster you could set its behaviour for life. Here are a few points to observe:

▸ Don't make loud noises or wave your arms to get your subject to look at the camera, as it could look very frightening from an animal's viewpoint. Be patient and get your pictures the ethical way.

▸ Don't treat the animal as a photographic subject: it is a living, breathing creature that shares our planet and should command as much respect as a human being.

▸ Be especially careful around mothers with young animals, as they will naturally be more nervous and protective and are likely to react aggressively to any unusual movements, sounds or smells.

▸ Always respect fragile habitats, ensure that you remain on official tracks and do not venture off-road without permission. Rules are there for a reason, either for your safety or that of the animal and its habitat. No picture is worth the degradation of the environment or putting an animal in danger. Tread carefully.

▸ Never hassle any animal or block its path. Always allow plenty of room for it to move away from you as and when it wants to, not when you decide you've had enough or want to get even closer.

Respect for Other Photographers

From time to time you may find yourself working in close proximity to other photographers and it is almost inevitable that conflicts will occur. It pays to remember that no photographer, amateur or professional, has any more rights (unless legally – see below) to photograph than you do. If someone has arrived at the best spot before you, then politely ask if you can join them and if you get more than just a grunt, slowly get into position so as not to disturb anything. If they flatly refuse to move, then you must move away and find something else to photograph. This is likely to make the other photographer think you are getting something great and eventually they will have to come and look. You will then have the right to take their place at the spot you originally wanted. Never move or drive in front of another photographer's shot just to get a look. This is a cardinal sin and will not endear you to anyone; bide your time and you will be rewarded.

Permits & Legal Permissions

Sometimes you will need an official permit for your wildlife photography, perhaps to drive off-road, to enter a very sensitive area or to photograph protected species. These permits can take two forms – either the official kind at the local government office or the folding money kind (aka a donation) to a local representative. Your local guides will know all about these. Make sure that your guides are reputable and check the potential for permits and licences before you travel, as you will need to budget for this too (another good reason for travelling as part of an organised tour). Visiting the country's embassy website can be helpful and should be part of your preparation before you go. Some zoos in Asia still charge a camera fee, so be honest and pay it, as your money will be probably go directly towards the upkeep of the very animals you are photographing.

Weasel lepilemur in tree nest, Réserve Privée de Berenty (Berenty Reserve), Madagascar
We found this lepilemur in its nest late one afternoon in the middle of a Madagascan rainforest. Since it is a very shy and almost exclusively nocturnal animal I refrained from using flash and took the minimum number of shots before leaving it completely alone.

▲ 35mm SLR, 300mm lens with 1.4x teleconverter, 1/250 f5.6, Provia 100F

Female lion with cub, Okavango Delta, Botswana

A mother with her young is always a great magnet for photographers and in Africa a lovely situation such as this can quickly attract a large collection of vehicles. If you are the first at the sighting, get your driver to park at the maximum distance that your biggest lens can cope with; this means that you are treating the animal with respect, will get your shots and, importantly, are setting the distance for everyone else (who might not be as responsible). Finally, concentrate on getting your shots and ignore everyone else and the temptation to swap stories – that is for the campfire!

▲ 35mm SLR, 300mm lens, 1/60 f8, Velvia 50

Polar bear walking on sea ice, Manitoba, Canada

Respecting the environment is something we can all do no matter what part of the world we are from or are visiting. We can help protect the environment by acting responsibly when travelling in wild areas and adhering to the old adage of only leaving footprints.

◀ 35mm DSLR, 500mm lens, 1/250 f4, ISO 200 RAW

PART FOUR

ON THE ROAD

Well, you've made it. You've arrived safe and sound and are eager to get going. The places, subjects and types of photographs you can take will be endless, so think carefully before setting foot in the field about what you would like to see and what sorts of images you really want to get. With luck, you'll be overwhelmed by photographic opportunities when out and about and, to maximise your chances of a great image or two, you will need to be quick to decide what your priorities are. The idea is to be in the right place at the right time and with the right light. Photographing wildlife is a game of chance to a large extent, but you do need to have some idea of what you want to achieve if you want Lady Luck to smile upon you.

Grizzly bear fishing, Alaska, USA
◄ DSLR, 300mm lens, 1/250 f5, ISO 200 RAW

ON SAFARI

Going on safari has never been more popular or accessible than it is today. The chance to get close to the 'Big Five' (elephant, rhino, buffalo, leopard and lion) exists nowhere except Africa. You can safari in whatever manner you wish, from staying in butler-serviced luxury lodges to roughing it in a tent. If your priority is photographing wildlife, make sure you choose an operator or guide with the same priority. Photography requires early mornings, late nights and a rather antisocial routine that may not be compatible with the group you're travelling with or the place where you are staying – do your research first.

When photographing on safari you will often be in a vehicle with other people and therefore will have to take the absolute minimum of equipment with you. A lens in the

African lion cub at sunrise, Masai Mara National Reserve, Kenya
Sunrise in Africa is such a special time and it is important to be out and about well beforehand (take a packed breakfast with you). I took this lion cub silhouette by using the techniques described on p78.
▲ DSLR, 70-200mm lens with 1.4x teleconverter, 1/1000 f4, ISO 200 RAW

Swallow-tailed bee-eater, Okavango Delta, Botswana

It is easy to forget about the spectacular bird life with all the big cats padding around, which is a shame as you will always see beautiful birds on safari. A fixed-focal-length lens will help isolate them from the background.

◀ 35mm SLR, 300mm lens with 1.4x teleconverter, 1/500 f5.6, Velvia 50

African leopard, Okavango Delta, Botswana

Seeing a leopard is top of everyone's list and it is a rare privilege when they show themselves enough to allow a clear picture. This one's appearance was such a surprise that I could barely fit it in the frame and wished I had a zoom!

◀ 35mm SLR, 500mm lens, 1/125 f4, Velvia 50

range of 100–400mm is perhaps the most useful for an SLR; for a compact a good zoom up to 8x will suffice. Tripods are impossible to use unless you are alone in a vehicle, so either use a monopod, get image-stabilised lenses (p104) and hand-hold them, or use a clamp and tripod head on the side of the vehicle. The key is to be flexible and always ready to shoot, as you never know what could be round the next corner. Keep your camera switched on at all times, with the lens cap off; a pillowcase can be useful to keep the dust from the camera and lens.

Working alongside others in the vehicle can occasionally be tense so ensure that everyone takes their turn at getting the shot, and change positions in the vehicle if some seats have more than their fair share of good views.

Male lion greeting cub, private game reserve, South Africa

Portraits of African wildlife are relatively easy to get, so always have your camera set up and ready for any interaction between predator and prey or family groups.

◀ DSLR, 500mm lens, 1/60 f4, ISO 200 RAW

African elephant feeding, Masai Mara National Reserve, Kenya

This isn't the greatest elephant picture I have taken but it illustrates a vital point – don't just take the angle that your driver gives you. Work out what you want and ask for it. In this instance I decided to put the vehicle below the ridge to show the elephant against the sky.

▼ DSLR, 300mm lens, 1/250 f5.6, ISO 100 RAW

IN THE RAINFOREST

There are several rainforest regions on this planet but perhaps the most frequently visited are the Amazon and those on the island of Madagascar. Working in a rainforest is a challenging task as you will be hot, sweaty and lunch for any small insect with wings. The wildlife is generally shy and reclusive and rarely gives you a second chance, which makes it all the more exciting and rewarding when you get a great shot. Rainforests are also about more than just wildlife – they contain diverse ecosystems which will capture the imaginations of even the most reluctant of macro photographers.

Black-and-white ruffed lemur, Madagascar
To get any light at all in rainforests it is best to concentrate on the areas close to forest clearings. I used a flash attached to an off-camera bracket and with a diffuser cup to create the soft light on the fur.
▲ 35mm SLR, 70-200mm lens with 1.4x teleconverter, 1/60 f5.6, Velvia 50, flash

Ocelot, Belize
If you are lucky enough to encounter some wildlife on the forest floor, don't be tempted to zoom in tight and get a facial shot; instead, take a wider angle view and show some of the dense vegetation that the animals call home.

◀ 35mm SLR, 300mm lens, 1/60 f4, Provia 100F, flash

Brazilian tapir, Brazil

If you have time and a camera to spare, then leaving a remotely triggered camera on a well-used jungle path can be a lot of fun. A warning though – animals are likely to damage the camera as they investigate it. Fortunately, on this occasion, the tapir left it alone.

◀ 35mm SLR, 28-80mm lens, 1/60 f11 manually set, Velvia 50, flash

For rainforest photography you will almost invariably be looking up into the canopy, so a flash is essential. Working in a rainforest is generally a tough, physical experience and a tripod can be a cumbersome accessory to take along. A monopod is a much better solution; ideally it should have a detachable tripod head mounted on top for those 'straight up' shots. For such shots, an eye-level finder will also save you from terminal back- and neck ache.

The light levels in most rainforests are low at best and so it pays to shoot at an ISO of 400 and above. Some of your subjects will be high in the canopy and a flash extender will bring them within range of your flash and help pick them out from the bright sky above. Take along a travel towel as the humidity will make you sweat all over your viewfinder and camera; some desiccant in your bag will also protect your cameras from the effects of excess humidity.

Common brown lemur, Mantady National Park, Madagascar

Don't be afraid to try something abstract, such as this image looking straight up – sometimes it really works! A wide-angle lens can give a real sense of the height of trees as well as the vertical extent of the rainforest.

◀ 35mm SLR, 17-35mm lens, 1/250 f5.6, Velvia 50

DESERT WILDLIFE

The world's desert regions are home to a surprising amount of wildlife, most of which only makes an appearance during the cool of the early mornings and late evenings. This means that the activity periods for your photography will be very short indeed, but the bonus is that you will always be shooting in beautiful light.

When shooting desert wildlife, it is a crime not to make the desert part of the picture. Try to visualise the scene before you take it; if your subject is walking, have it leading into the picture and try to use prominent natural features to frame the shot.

Namaqua chameleon, Namib Desert, Namibia
This is one of my favourite desert images. We found this chap walking about in 49°C (120°F) heat searching for food. It's the stark habitat that marks this image as something different.
▲ 645 SLR, 200mm lens, 1/800 f5.6, Velvia 50

Eastern diamondback rattle-snake, Arizona, USA

Desert wildlife can be dangerous and several times I have almost come a cropper with snakes. The only policy with them is to be safe and photograph from a long way away (the moon is not far enough in my opinion) and with a guide who knows exactly what they are doing.
◀ 35mm SLR, 500mm lens with extension tube, 1/250 f4, Velvia 50

African leopard tracks, Namib Desert, Namibia
Often, tracks are all you can see in a desert, but don't dismiss them as a waste of time. If photographed correctly they can make cracking shots. I shot these leopard tracks into the light and leading from one edge of the frame to make it a little more interesting. I never found the culprit but *c'est la vie!*

▲ 35mm SLR, 17-35mm lens, 1/60 f11, Velvia 50

SEA-BIRD COLONIES

The great attraction of a sea-bird colony for the photographer is the sheer abundance of action and picture opportunities. The air is full of wheeling birds, challenging your skills to the limit, and every available nook and cranny has some species of sea bird lurking.

A neat trick is to try a really bold composition and get a foreground bird as large as possible on one side of the frame. This creates foreground interest for the viewer and naturally leads their eye to the action going on in the rest of the image. Although it is tempting to use a large depth of field to get everything in sharp focus, be careful not to use much

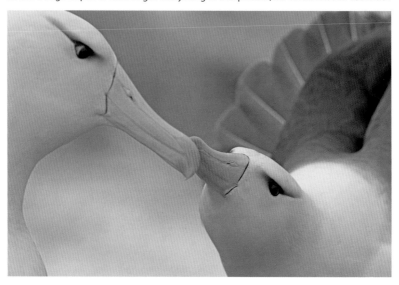

Black-browed albatross pair bonding, Falkland Islands
Courtship rituals between sea birds are very advanced affairs. These albatrosses performed this ritual each time one returned to the nest, so I had plenty of time to get it right. I used a fill-in flash to place a nice highlight in the eyes; this is often a useful accessory with sea birds as their eyes tend to be dark. The disadvantage of using flash is that most sea birds have some white feathers which can be easily overexposed, so use a diffuser cup to cut the power right down.
▲ DSLR, 300mm lens, 1/60 f8, ISO 100 RAW

Gannets landing at colony, Bass Rock, Scotland

Portraits of sea birds in isolation may be beautiful but do little to convey the noise and chaos of a typical colony. When trying this kind of shot it's important to get a strong foreground element to put the whole image in context. You may know what the small dots in the picture are but it's a good bet that anyone else looking at it will be confused. I used a super wide-angle lens and a polariser, and composed the shot to include some nesting birds.

◀ 35mm SLR, 28-80mm lens, 1/125 f8, Provia 100F, polarising filter

above f11, as the foreground subject must stand out enough to be interesting in itself. Lens choice here is all-important: use a 70-200mm for this job as it will provide a degree of isolation for the foreground subject while giving enough depth for the background. A super wide-angle lens, such as a 17mm, can create a superb effect, but for this to work you generally have to be right up against the nostrils of your subject. While most sea birds are remarkably tolerant, it does pay to show them some respect (especially if they are on a nest) and keep out of squirting range (sometimes from both ends)!

Puffin taking off, Skomer Island, Wales
Light plays an important factor in any sea-bird colony and I always look for unexpected angles. With this image I shot slightly into the light, with the dark background provided by a cliff in shadow.
▲ 35mm SLR, 70-200mm lens, 1/250 f5.6, Velvia 50

Steamer duck, Falkland Islands
The most difficult shot in a sea-bird colony is getting a single bird in isolation. The best idea is to head for the edge of the colony and look for an outcrop where several birds are perching. Use a low aperture of f5.6 to isolate the sea bird from the background and shoot from a low angle, especially if you are lucky enough to have a blue sky or dark, stormy skies.
◀ DSLR, 300mm lens, 1/250 f5.6, ISO 50 RAW

AROUND WATER

Water is the lifeblood of the animal kingdom. All mammals must come to drink, so a water hole in a desert can be a real hot spot of activity and lurking close by will often yield great results. Ponds, lakes and rivers are also incredibly productive for photographing bird and insect life, and rarely would you leave such an area without any shots.

The Holy Grail for water shots is the reflection on the water, and there are a few tricks you can use to maximise the effect if you see a likely shot:

▸ If the light permits, set the aperture to f8 and lock the focus directly onto the subject's eyes. This will not only make the subject 100% sharp but will also give a little extra sharpness to the reflection in the water.

▸ The best reflections are moody ones, so make sure you underexpose the image slightly by setting the exposure compensation to –2/3.

▸ Unless the composition screams out for a landscape orientation, turn the camera and shoot with a portrait (vertical) format to lead the reflection away from the subject.

▸ Since animals are at their most vulnerable when drinking, they will also look up. Be prepared for this as you'll get a cascade of water droplets from their open mouths; shoot with a high shutter speed to freeze the drops in mid air.

▸ Time your image carefully to capture a shot of the animal's tongue: do not rely on the motor drive to do it for you or you will miss the shot.

Black-backed jackal drinking, Savuti, Botswana

Shot at first light, this was a completely opportunistic encounter with the jackal – proof that being ready at all times pays dividends.

◂ 35mm SLR, 600mm lens, 1/125 f4, Provia 100F

Great blue heron, the Everglades, USA

Getting the focus right can be a real challenge when your subject is moving; fortunately this heron had paused and was watching the water ahead for a potential meal.

▲ 35mm SLR, 300mm lens, 1/500 f5.6, Velvia 50

Tricolor heron, the Everglades, USA

I love photographing moody exposures such as this; the only problem is that you can never plan for it. The combination of black water and raking morning light gives this image a very simple feeling and made getting up two hours before dawn very worthwhile.

▲ 35mm SLR, 300mm lens with 1.4x teleconverter, 1/125 f4, Velvia 50

Hippos at sunrise, Waterberg, South Africa

I had passed this spot on several mornings before the hippos were finally in the right position. It is a very peaceful image, with the morning light made slightly more saturated by some deliberate underexposure.

◀ 35mm SLR, 300mm lens, 1/350 f5.6, Velvia 50

FROM THE AIR

Photographing wildlife from the air provides some great opportunities to get an alternative view of the natural world. The species in question usually needs to be on the large side too and completely in the open; pictures of blue whales in the ocean work much better than a brown bear on a rocky landscape would, because the whale's colour makes a contrast against its background. It's a great way of photographing herds of animals, as the

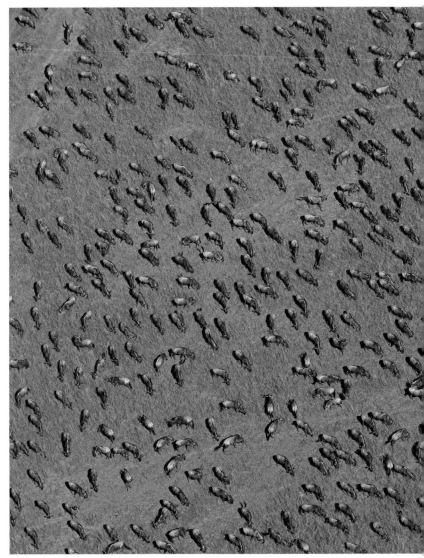

examples below show. When photographing from the air you have two choices: through a window or through an open door. The latter is only for experienced photographers and should be undertaken only if you are fully harnessed and flying with a pilot who is very experienced at working in this way. Most of your aerial photography is likely to be through a window and this can work well, particularly with the type of window that lifts up in flight. If shooting through a window, make sure you place your lens directly against the glass to cut down any reflections.

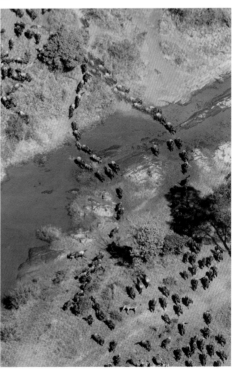

Common wildebeest crossing river, Masai Mara National Reserve, Kenya

Overcoming the problem of ground speed is perhaps the greatest challenge to the aerial photographer, because the closer you are to the ground the faster it will rush by. A shutter speed of 1/500 will usually give you sharp results. The shape of the wildebeest crossing the river has made this a favourite image of mine.

▲ DSLR, 70-200mm lens with 1.4x teleconverter, 1/500 f11, ISO 200 RAW

Common wildebeest on plains, Masai Mara National Reserve, Kenya

Composition is crucial with aerial photography; look for interesting shapes or ground patterns to include in your pictures and always try to fly early or late in the day. This very odd image shows a herd of wildebeest feeding before attempting a river crossing during their annual migration.

◀ DSLR, 70-200mm lens with 1.4x teleconverter, 1/350 f11, ISO 200 RAW

ZOOS & WILDLIFE SANCTUARIES

Zoos and wildlife sanctuaries provide great places to photograph wildlife that you may not be able to see in the wild. Some zoos are better than others, but standards are improving worldwide and most zoos now offer some good opportunities, which is excellent for those photographers who are not fortunate enough to travel. If you are travelling, however, and find yourself at a loose end for a day, check out the local zoo – it will rarely disappoint.

It might seem that photographing in a zoo is easy because you don't have to find the animals. This may be true but you still have to use all of your technical skill (and patience) to get shots to be proud of.

Timing

Most animals are at their most active first thing in the morning and last thing at night; the latter is usually feeding time and they will be very active in the 30 minutes or so beforehand. Once they have been fed, forget it – they will sleep for several hours with a contented smile on their faces.

Caracal, Marwell Zoo, England

Zoos can also allow you to get close to young animals that would be hidden in the wild, such as this young caracal. You would be extremely lucky to see one of these very shy animals in the wild. Finding the right angle to photograph the subject can mean that you can get superb portraits even in an enclosure.

◄ 35mm SLR, 100-400mm lens, 1/500 f5.6, Provia 100F

Composition

Look for unusual angles and do not just take the easy shot. Use a long lens to isolate the subjects and help remove any inorganic elements from the image.

Shooting Through Wire

There is no magical way of removing wire from your shots (apart from manipulating them later) but you can use a very small depth of field (f4 to f5.6) to minimise their impact. Try to pick an area where the wire is in shadow, as that will help mask it; trying to shoot through brand new silver wire in bright sunlight is a total waste of time.

Reticulated giraffe, Marwell Zoo, England

Look for unusual angles – don't just go for the boring shot. Some zoos organise special feeding sessions so you can get classic shots just like this. One piece of advice – don't get your lens licked as it could destroy the protective coating.

▲ DSLR, 17-35mm lens, 1/60 f11, ISO 100 RAW, flash

Asian elephants, Pinnewala Elephant Orphanage, Sri Lanka

Some wildlife orphanages are world-famous and welcome photographers. This image was taken at the Pinnewala Elephant Orphanage, a brilliant place for photography. When working in such places, try to capture your subjects exhibiting natural behaviour, and avoid manufactured objects.

◀ DSLR, 70-200mm lens, 1/60 f5.6, ISO 100 RAW

Shooting Through Glass

Some modern zoos have glass enclosures that are great for photography. A lens hood is vital here to cut down reflections – place it flat against the glass. If you are using a compact with a built-in flash, it is vital that you hold the lens flat to the glass. With an external flash it is also best that you hold it flat to the glass so the beam is not reflected back into the flash sensor; this causes premature shut-off and therefore underexposure.

Young meerkat, Marwell Zoo, England

Just as it is important to shoot in good light in the field, it is equally important in a zoo. Check the position of the sun in relation to the enclosures to enhance your chances of getting well-lit images. I took this shot of a young meerkat in the last few minutes of light at the end of the day.

◀ DSLR, 300mm lens, 1/60 f4, ISO 200 RAW

White rhinoceros, Knowsley Safari Park, England

As well as feeding sessions, some zoos hold special photographic days when, under the supervision of a keeper, you can get your lenses through the wire. To get this shot I used a super wide-angle lens resting on the ground to give a powerful effect.

◀ DSLR, 17-35mm lens, 1/320 f8, ISO 100 RAW

Sun bear, Zoo Negara, Malaysia
There are some animals that would be impossible to photograph in the wild and so a captive collection or zoo is the only way to capture them. As with animals in the wild, do your research first so that you can appreciate the animals' characteristics. In this case it was the long tongue of this sun bear.

▲ 35mm SLR, 100-400mm lens, 1/125 f5.6, Provia 100F

PORTRAITS

Everyone loves close-up images. Animals really lend themselves to shots that fill the frame, especially if they are colourful. Bear the following in mind when composing the shot:

▶ If you have a zoom lens, frame the image from the neck up, and do not include any legs in the frame.

▶ Try to get the neck in a bottom corner of the image and the head in the centre, as this leads the viewer's eye naturally to the head and gives the image a good balance.

▶ Keep a sharp focus on the eyes: they are naturally any animal's focal point.

▶ Use an aperture of f5.6 to f8 to be sure of getting the nose and ears in sharp focus while keeping the background diffuse.

▶ Wait until the subject looks up – there is nothing worse than getting shadows covering the eyes and turning the animal into an alien.

▶ For the same reason, shoot in low light or on a cloudy day; in bright sunlight you will struggle to see the eyes.

Lowland gorilla, Port Lympne Wild Animal Park, England
Tight facial portraits like this work brilliantly with primates as they are so expressive. To enhance the mood I deliberately shot the image on the dark side (in cloudy conditions), and during processing converted it to black and white.

▲ DSLR, 300mm lens, 1/200 f11, ISO 100 RAW

Green-winged macaws, the Pantanal, Brazil

Sometimes an intimate portrait can involve more than one animal – perhaps the tender moments between a mother and young. In this case it was the courtship between two green-winged macaws. I chose a portrait format mainly to ensure that their tails were not cut off.

▶ 35mm SLR, 500mm lens, 1/125 f8, Provia 100F

Rockhopper penguin, Falkland Islands

In this image I wanted to give the portrait a little space and have a hint of the sea behind, albeit miles out of focus. The main difficulty was the exposure, as it proved very difficult to get the balance right between the black-and-white plumage without burning out the white feathers. In the end I simply took a reading from a neutral point, as described on p57.

▲ DSLR, 300mm lens, 1/500 f8, ISO 100 RAW

African leopard, private game reserve, South Africa

Direct eye contact works well for big cats, but the cardinal sin is to get 'half-moon' eyes. To ensure you can see all of their eyes, you need to shoot in very early, very late or overcast light and take a low angle, since they obviously do not enjoy looking directly at the sun.

▲ DSLR, 300mm lens, 1/125 f6.7, ISO 100 RAW

EXPRESSIONS

Most mammals have the same variety of facial expressions that we do: interest, fear and anger are three emotions that appear more often than anything else. Primates are undoubtedly the masters of the facial expression and will never disappoint you.

Most pictures showing expressions will be in extreme close-up, as you want the main focus to be on a single animal. This usually means using your longest focal length. If you have a zoom, always try to use it at its longest range. This will blur the background and therefore place the main focus of the image on the animal's face. Get the focus squarely between the eyes by careful selection of the focus point, and use an aperture of f5.6 to f8 (f11 if it is looking straight at the camera) to ensure that the important bits are in focus.

Chimpanzee posing, Zambia

No discussion about expressions would be complete without a primate image, as primates undoubtedly have the greatest range of expressions in the animal kingdom. Capturing them is simply a question of time in the field – spend long enough there and they will show you a wide range of expressions.

◀ 35mm SLR, 28-80mm lens, 1/320 f8, Velvia 50

African leopard sleeping, Masai Mara National Reserve, Kenya

Expressions can be peaceful too; the feeling of relaxation and contentment on this leopard's face is obvious to all. I used natural light for this shot and avoided flash at all costs, as I didn't want to disturb the leopard's slumber.

▲ DSLR, 300mm lens with 1.4x teleconverter, 1/500 f5.6, ISO 100 RAW

Black bear snarling, Montana, USA

I always shy away from using flash, but sometimes it can make a real difference by adding some much-needed light. Here it created a huge contrast between the jaws and the head while illuminating the throat (which I wasn't tempted to see any closer), leading to an interesting image created on a very dull, overcast day.

▲ 35mm SLR, 300mm lens, 1/125 f5.6, Provia 100F, flash

Red deer roaring in rut, Scotland

Most pictures showing expressions will be in extreme close-up, as you want the main focus to be on the individual animal. Here I placed the autofocus point squarely over the eyes and used an aperture of f8 to keep everything in sharp focus; shooting with a 500mm fixed-focal-length lens helped keep the background diffuse.

▲ DSLR, 500mm lens, 1/250 f8, ISO 400 RAW

Caiman snapping jaws, the Pantanal, Brazil

This image took me completely by surprise and I had the shutter speed set quite low – hence the blur on the lower jaw. I think the motion adds to the final image, but as a rule, for snarling or yawning animals you will need a decent shutter speed (above 1/250) to freeze the motion.

◀ 35mm SLR, 28-80mm lens, 1/60 f11, Velvia 50

RELATIONSHIPS

One of the attractions of wildlife photography is that provides you with many different opportunities to show the relationships that occur in the natural world. All species, even those with solitary lives, at some time come into contact with others. Documenting the relationships between them can yield remarkable results. It doesn't matter what the relationship is, either: the bond between a mother and her young, the struggle between predator and prey, or two youngsters playing.

Composition plays a much greater role in this kind of image than any technical considerations. If you are taking family images then the closer you can get to the subject the better; whereas for a predator and its prey you should take a wider-angle view to put the scene into context.

Bengal tigers, Bandhavgarh National Park, India

A lovely moment as two siblings greeted each other was almost ruined when the elephant I was sitting on chose that moment to shift its weight. For the 75 millionth time in my career my image-stabilised lens saved my bacon.

◀ 35mm SLR, 100-400mm lens, 1/250 f8, Provia 100F

Hyacinth macaws, the Pantanal, Brazil
Hyacinth macaws are real characters and will always reward patience with a good shot like this.
▲ 35mm SLR, 500mm lens, 1/200 f8, Velvia 50

Masai giraffe cleaning young, Masai Mara National Reserve, Kenya
The interaction between mother and young is always special. We waited with this giraffe family for a whole morning to record these tender moments. Giraffes with young are among the most difficult compositions as there is such a size difference; the trick is to keep your camera on the youngster, because that is where all the action will be centred.
◀ DSLR, 100-400mm lens, 1/250 f8, ISO 100 RAW

HABITATS

Many photographers are happy taking intimate portraits of wild animals and rarely think of including the habitat. This is a shame as the habitat is often as beautiful as the subject itself, if not more so. Taking a wider view can also introduce mood and a sense of wilderness and can transform your image into a picture rather than a snapshot. Many photographers make prints of their work, especially for the home, and a habitat-style shot will be much easier to enjoy; a wider-angle image is more in the style of the great wildlife artists, who rarely paint full frame and could teach photographers a few lessons about composition.

▸ Try to compose the shot to have the subject leading or walking into the picture rather than out of it.

▸ Although you want to include the background in the shot, it is important not to lose the subject in it. It still pays to keep the aperture at f5.6 to f8.

▸ The habitat shot only works if the subject is either equal to or brighter than the background. If the background is much brighter, it will create an imbalance in the image and be distracting.

Cattle egrets roosting, the Pantanal, Brazil
I had passed this roost on several nights on my way back to the lodge before I saw the image I wanted. The last light cast a beautiful glow over the roosting egrets and I deliberately shot the image to include the river, as that was part of the story.

◀ 35mm SLR, 100-400mm lens, 1/60 f8, Provia 100F

Springbok herd in thunderstorm, Namib Desert, Namibia
Light can make or break habitat shots. We came across this herd of springbok bathed in strong sunlight, while the mountains above were receiving a deluge of rain. The composition was obvious since the mountain had such strong diagonals and the springboks were in such lovely light.

▲ DSLR, 100-400mm lens, 1/60 f11, ISO 100 RAW

Gentoo penguins on landing beach, Falkland Islands
My goal here was to combine the traditional elements of a landscape picture (foreground interest) with the added interest of some penguins on their way home.
▲ DSLR, 17-35mm lens, 1/60 f22, ISO 100 RAW, polarising filter

Black grouse, Northumberland, England
Taking a low angle can really help to improve composition and will give a totally different feel to the shot. Taken at sunrise, this displaying male black grouse was taken from inside a very low hide with the camera resting on a beanbag; I used an angle finder (see p35) to save my back!
▲ DSLR, 300mm lens, 1/125 f5.6, ISO 200 RAW

ABSTRACTS

Experimentation is good for you and will improve your photography and give diversity to your collection of images. Always look for something slightly different and do not be constrained by the traditionalists of wildlife photography. Many species have beautiful fur, skin, patterns or feathers, so don't be afraid to compose your shot using any of these elements as the central part of the image.

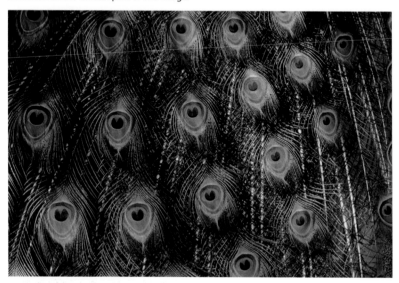

Peacock feathers, Yala National Park, Sri Lanka
Plumage and feathers can be really colourful and will make a good abstract image.
▲ DSLR, 70-200mm lens with 1.4x teleconverter, 1/250 f8, ISO 100 RAW

European brown bear, eastern Finland
When I am working in the field, I try to take a complete life story of my subject, photographing it from different angles and in different light. This always includes abstracts and I couldn't resist it when this bear placed its paws on one side of the tree while licking sap from the other side.
◄ DSLR, 17-35mm lens, 1/60 f22, ISO 100 RAW, polarising filter

African elephant, MalaMala Game Reserve, South Africa
The rough skin of an elephant provides a wonderful opportunity for an abstract. It is best shot slightly into the sun and in early or late light to accentuate the shadows.

▲ DSLR, 300mm lens, 1/60 f8, ISO 100 RAW

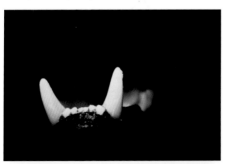

Jaguar teeth, Belize
A real abstract: the black-coloured jaguar was in such deep shade that a standard image was impossible. The teeth, however, shone out, so I shot this abstract image and converted it to black and white on my PC.

◀ DSLR, 100-400mm lens, 1/60 f5.6, ISO 400 RAW

Jaguar markings, Belize
If you are shooting a macro-style image, try to look for patterns within a bird's plumage or the superb markings on a mammal's coat. This image works because of the patterns and also the transition between high colour and dark shadowy areas. Try to use an aperture of f8 to get everything in relatively sharp focus, and increase this to f11 or more if you are photographing something that is not relatively flat and parallel to the camera.

◀ 35mm SLR, 500mm lens with 1.4x teleconverter, 1/400 f8, Velvia 50

BIG CATS

Big cats are perhaps the most photographed species on our planet. To photograph big cats successfully you will need to be completely obsessed by them and completely focused on getting the shots that you want. This means that you'll need to go specifically to a hot spot and work intensively on the ground. Many people will be lucky enough to encounter big cats on their travels as part of a mixed location trip, but you will still need to dedicate some time to them and forget all other distractions.

Big cats are only active for very short periods of the day, which is usually limited to a couple of hours in the morning and an hour in the evening. In the cool of the morning all big cats will generally be active to some degree; either hunting, socialising or just walking along their territorial boundaries. As the day moves on and it gets hotter, they will seek shade and then sleep soundly for most of the day. When it is very hot, they may not move from the shade until dusk, which can be a source of great frustration if you've sat with them for several hours. Consequently, the morning is perhaps the peak time and it's essential to be well prepared for your photography:

▸ **Time** It is essential that you look for cats well before the first rays of the sun light up the landscape. This time of the morning is magical and any big cat looks stunning in those first few minutes of red light. The only way you can get these shots is to find the cats in the pre-dawn light and stay with them through the first hour of light.

▸ **Be prepared** Have your cameras switched on and ready to shoot at all times. Keep the camera switched on, with a new, fully charged battery, an empty memory card or new film, exposure set to aperture priority (AV) f5.6 (to pick a fast shutter speed) and autofocus to servo/tracking. The latter is very important as you'll often comes across a big cat moving and in all the excitement you may accidentally forget to change your autofocus from one shot to tracking. Since the tonality in that first hour of light is so good, your exposures should be fine if left to the meter, especially if evaluative metering is chosen.

▸ **Composition** Don't just go for the straight portrait; try to vary your photography to make the most of the light. Look at different angles for the sunrise. Backlit shots can work really well and you may get the ring-of-fire effect. The sky at this time of the day is also beautiful so don't be afraid to incorporate it in a wide-angle environmental portrait.

African lion, Okavango Delta, Botswana

The faces of big cats make fantastic abstracts and some, like lions, are so tolerant of approach that you can get shots like this without any personal danger. This shot only works because of the low light and the fact that the whole of the eye is visible; any shadow would ruin it completely. Images like this need to be sharp from edge to edge, so use a high aperture, such as f8 or f11.

◂ 35mm SLR, 300mm lens with 1.4x teleconverter, 1/125 f8, Velvia 50

Bengal tiger sleeping, Bandhavgarh National Park, India
Some big cats seem to spend their whole time sleeping. This tiger didn't wake up in the 2½ hours that I spent with him. Still, it made a nice shot.
▲ 35mm SLR, 100-400mm lens, 1/250 f5.6, Provia 100F

In the sheer excitement of seeing a big cat you may get so engrossed by your photography that you accidentally forget the number-one rule of wildlife photography – respect. It is far better to use a long lens and sit far away from a big cat than it is to crowd it; in the latter scenario, it will not be relaxed and your angle of photography will be down rather than horizontal. Cats rarely look up and you'll end up with images of half-open eyes that will only be good for the recycle bin. Also, don't hassle your driver to go off-road after the cat, as off-road driving seriously damages the habitat. You may act responsibly and have the best of intentions, but the van-loads of camera-waving, Hawaiian-shirted tourists who follow you may not. It's not worth risking damage to the environment for the sake of a picture – don't forget that the animals have to live there.

African lion cubs, Masai Mara National Reserve, Kenya
Cute is always appealing and young cats are some of the most adorable. These two young lion cubs are no exception. Being so small, these two were soaked through by the heavy dew. Damp conditions are always worth photographing in, as the light with moisture in the air is astounding.
◀ DSLR, 300mm lens, 1/750 f4, ISO 200 RAW

African leopard hunting, private game reserve, South Africa

Leopards are renowned for their amazingly patterned coats which are designed to enable them to lurk in the shadows when hunting. It's when they're hunting that leopards look their best, as this portrait shot shows. The best time to catch leopards on the ground and see them in their full glory is very early in the morning or very late in the day.

◀ DSLR, 300mm lens, 1/500 f4, ISO 200 RAW

Cheetah mother washing cub, Masai Mara National Reserve, Kenya

Cheetahs are reasonably antisocial animals, except when they have cubs. Spending time with an individual or family is worth its weight in gold when you are rewarded with intimate images such as this.

▼ DSLR, 500mm lens, 1/250 f5.6, ISO 200 RAW

Clouded leopard, private sanctuary, England
There are many big cats on the highly endangered list, including the clouded leopard. For many photographers the only opportunity to photograph such beautiful animals is in captivity at a local zoo or sanctuary.

▲ 35mm SLR, 70-200mm lens, 1/125 f8, Provia 100F

BEARS

There are many species of bears throughout the world but perhaps the most popular for the travelling wildlife photographer are the polar, grizzly and black bears. Today, bear-watching is a big industry and there are several destinations that offer guaranteed encounters and therefore great opportunities for photography. The most famous is undoubtedly the town of Churchill in Canada, which for six weeks from early October each year is the location of a major pilgrimage for polar-bear enthusiasts worldwide.

Grizzly bear, Alaska, USA

Pounding through the river chasing a salmon, this grizzly was an awesome sight. To capture it I selected all the autofocus points, used servo/tracking autofocus and wore cast-iron underpants.

◄ DSLR, 300mm lens, 1/750 f4, ISO 200 RAW

Grizzly bear, Alaska, USA

Bears never fail to give great opportunities for the camera; this one is taking a much-earned rest after a hard afternoon's fishing. I know just how he feels!

◄ DSLR, 500mm lens with 1.4x teleconverter, 1/125 f8, ISO 400 RAW

Polar bear mother and cubs, Churchill, Canada

Some experiences as a wildlife photographer will stay with you forever, as this will for us. Spending two days with a mother and cubs, just out from their den, was a rare privilege.

◀ 35mm SLR, 500mm lens with 1.4x teleconverter, 1/125 f8, Velvia 50

Bear photography is usually an opportunistic pastime and the activity you will see depends entirely on the season. For example, in the early part of the summer you will see grizzly bears engaged in courtship activities. As the season progresses they turn their total attention to the salmon migration, which can lead to spectacular pictures. Bears are notoriously unpredictable and will usually reveal how they are feeling towards you with a series of body postures. These can be difficult to read, so when in bear country it is essential to travel with a local skilled expert.

Grizzly bear, Alaska, USA

This sow caught the salmon right in front of us – the highlight of any grizzly photographic adventure – and proceeded to bring it towards us. I used servo/tracking autofocus to keep her sharply in focus.

▲ DSLR, 300mm lens, 1/250 f4, ISO 200 RAW

Black bear, Minnesota, USA

Black bears are a nightmare to photograph, as their fur absorbs so much light. The camera light meter is always hopelessly wrong so use the techniques described on p57.

▲ 35mm SLR, 300mm lens, 1/250 f5.6, Velvia 50

PRIMATES

Primates inhabit the world's forested areas and are generally very elusive. The most common encounters between primates and humans are either at camp sites or at established feeding sites. These feeding sites present good opportunities for photography but you will generally have to be quick, as primates are the smash-and-grab merchants of the animal kingdom. If you do get yourself into close proximity to primates, they are surprisingly easy to photograph, especially in the case of orang-utans, chimpanzees and gorillas. Their facial expressions are amazing and the main target for any budding primate photographer. To capture them you will need a reasonably long lens, as you want the composition to centre on the face. You will also need a flash, mounted off-camera to avoid red eye, as most primates have a lot of facial shadow and very black eyes. The exception is the chimpanzee, whose eyes can only be described as soulful.

Snow monkey sleeping, Nagano, Japan

The main problem with this image was keeping the lens free of steam, as the snow monkey was sleeping on the edge of a geothermal pool. An off-camera flash with a diffuser cup, set to a very reduced power, created the soft light on the face.

▲ 35mm SLR, 70-200mm lens, 1/125 f5.6, Velvia 50, flash

Chimpanzee, Chimfunshi Wildlife Orphanage, Zambia

Primates with young are always a challenge, as their natural instinct is, understandably, to protect their young from prying lenses. So I always try to use a long lens to keep the mother relaxed. It worked here as I managed to capture the young chimpanzee looking out from the safety of its mother's embrace.

◀ 35mm SLR, 500mm lens, 1/250 f4, Velvia 50

Orang-utan, Tanjung Puting National Park, Indonesian Borneo

Orang-utans have a wide range of expressions, and with time it is easy to capture them. A small amount of fill-in flash was used to provide highlights in the eyes and I deliberately used both arms to lead from each corner to create a very structured composition.

◀ 35mm SLR, 100-400mm lens, 1/60 f5.6, Provia 100F, flash

Orang-utan youngsters, Sepilok Nature Resort, Malaysian Borneo

Rehabilitation centres often encourage tourists as a vital source of income and can be a wonderful opportunity to get close to primates. I was fortunate enough to go to just such a centre at playtime when the youngsters were up to all kinds of mischief.

◀ 35mm SLR, 28-80mm lens, 1/60 f8, Velvia 50, flash

SEALS

If sea birds are the fun subjects of the bird world then marine mammals are their mammalian equivalents. By far the most common and accessible are seals. Most seals live in well-established colonies. A seal colony assails the senses, especially the nose, like no other and it is relatively easy to great wildlife shots without any real effort. Most seals are notoriously difficult to approach and will scuttle off into the sea at the slightest sight of you on the horizon. The one time of the year when they will not is the pupping season, when numbers will be at their peak and photographic opportunities abound.

Seals need to be treated with extreme respect, especially huge elephant seals that weigh over a tonne. If scared, seals will immediately seek the safety of the sea and will go through anything in their way to get there; this is one reason you should never get between them and the sea. Another area to be careful of is a mother with her pup; all mothers are protective and this is their most stressful period of the year. Therefore mothers with pups need to be approached with extreme caution and should always be shot from a low angle (which will serve to mask your body shape) with your biggest lens. So keep your distance – a minimum of 15m is usually sufficient and will keep everyone happy.

The obvious shots to look for in a seal colony are tight facial portraits and action shots. With the former, it pays to get a low angle and use an aperture of f8 to keep the area from the nose to the eyes in sharp focus. Wet seals are an exposure nightmare, but fortunately there are usually many neutral reference points such as sand or rocks close by for you to take a meter reading from. Try to get a variety of shots, keep your eyes peeled for any fights brewing in the water and enjoy yourself – seals are highly entertaining!

Grey seal being aggressive, Lincolnshire, England

Seals have very expressive and 'characterful' faces and make great subjects for tight portraits. I shot this with an aperture of f8 to ensure I had sufficient depth of field.

◀ 35mm SLR, 300mm lens with 1.4x teleconverter, 1/125 f8, Provia 100F

Northern elephant seal bull, California, USA

Don't get between a seal and the water – I cannot say this enough. This huge elephant seal put on a surprising turn of speed when it spotted a rival on the beach and it gave me new respect for their speed on the ground. Don't get caught – it will hurt.

◀ 35mm SLR, 500mm lens, 1/60 f5.6, Velvia 50

Harp seal pup, Îles de la Madeleine (Magdalen Islands), Canada

Seal cubs are always photogenic no matter what species they are, and this harp seal is probably the cutest of the lot. Exposure was difficult in this location as I had no neutral reference points and this, coupled with the seal, snow and ice, caused the camera meter to underexpose all the time. So I relied on the old sunny f16 rule: 1/125 at f16 on ISO 100. I could also have simply metered directly from the seal and added between +1 and +1½ stops exposure compensation.

▲ 35mm SLR, 28-80mm lens, 1/125 f16, Provia 100F

Grey seals fighting, Northumberland, England

Fights are common in seal colonies, and if you lurk around for long enough one will be sure to occur.

◄ 35mm SLR, 500mm lens, 1/500 f5.6, Provia 100F

BIRDS

Birds are fabulous photographic subjects and can be found anywhere in the world. They have endless combinations of type, colour and behaviour and live in all sorts of locations. Most bird images are likely to involve the sky to some extent. If you are lucky enough to have sunny conditions, you can use the blue sky as a backdrop, which will create a wonderful contrast for any feathers. If the weather is cloudy, however, it is essential that you avoid using the sky at all costs and position yourself so that you can use a neutral-coloured solid backdrop, such as a forest. This may entail you climbing a little higher or taking a bit more care when getting into position, but the results will be more than worth it.

Birds in Flight

There can be no more spectacular sight than a skein of geese taking off at sunrise or an owl swooping down on its prey. Images of birds in flight are the essence of bird photography, and capturing the full beauty and artistry of flight with your camera requires an artistic eye as well as just technical skill.

Flight photography is one area of wildlife photography where being artistic can yield frighteningly good results. The basic idea is to use a slow shutter speed in order to blur the motion of the bird's wings and thereby show the beauty of flight. Although these shots are preconceived, taking them is very much a hit-and-miss affair and most of them end up occurring by accident. If you have a DSLR then there is no problem as you can quickly delete unsuccessful images; however, for 35mm film users it's a gamble and for medium-format users it's a very expensive gamble. Of course some subjects (such as the crane on the opposite page) lend themselves to this more than others – the more

Barn owl, Hampshire, England
The moment of takeoff is a great opportunity to photograph birds, and careful observation will show you when a bird is likely to go. Quite often birds will preen or appear agitated immediately prior to takeoff, so watch for those signs carefully and you will be rewarded – if you are quick enough!

▲ DSLR, 300mm lens with 1.4x teleconverter, 1/1000 f4, ISO 200 RAW

Whooper swan flock flying in to roost, Norfolk, England
Since all the front birds were roughly in line, I selected all the autofocus points with servo/tracking autofocus for this lovely shot.
▲ DSLR, 70-200mm lens with 1.4x teleconverter, 1/350 f11, ISO 200 RAW

elegant (and slow) the wing beat, the more artistic the effect. For images like this, a good starting point is to use a shutter speed of between 1/15 and 1/30, with your autofocus set to servo/tracking mode. Using a flash with second-curtain synchronisation (p30) will also give great effects.

Takeoff

Framing a potential takeoff is all-important; you need to compose the image to have the bird on one side so that it has space in the image to move into when it takes off. Therefore it is vital that you avoid cropping in too tight, so as not to end up with bird

Japanese crane, Hokkaido, Japan

When photographing birds, watch out for potentially artistic movements. Birds are some of the most graceful creatures on the planet and flight lends itself to artistic blurring and panning techniques, as this image of a Japanese crane in flight clearly shows.

◀ 35mm SLR, 300mm lens, 1/30 f8, Velvia 50, tripod

pictures with chopped-off wings. This is why a zoom is so useful. The autofocus needs to be switched to servo/tracking mode, with the bird as the initial point of focus. When it moves either take a sequence of images as it flies across the frame or pan the camera and follow its motion. A shutter speed of 1/1000 will usually be enough to freeze motion, which in turn will always give a low aperture of f4 to f5.6. This is desirable because a small depth of field will remove any distracting backgrounds and allow the subject to be the main focus of the image.

Landing

The easiest of all flight shots, images of birds landing simply require that you select all the autofocus points in servo/tracking mode and follow the motion of the bird as it comes in to land. Be careful not to fire too early as you might fill the DSLR buffer up too soon; it is better to wait until the bird is about to touch down with feet fully outstretched (especially if it is on water).

Great black-backed gull, western coast, Norway

Using its wings to slow its speed, this gull landed right next to my boat. An image-stabilised lens helped me keep steady in the vital moments.

◀ DSLR, 300mm lens, 1/200 f8, ISO 100 RAW

White-tailed sea eagle, western coast, Norway

Good flight shots require something more than just the bird to make them stand out from the crowd. In this case the stormy sky adds to the drama of the picture.

▲ DSLR, 300mm lens, 1/250 f5.6, ISO 200 RAW

PENGUINS

Penguins are found across the length and breadth of the Antarctic continent and on the sub-Antarctic islands that surround it. They are the star attraction on any Antarctic cruise and will never disappoint as photographic subjects. For most travellers the opportunities for penguin photography will be short and sweet, as you will be given a few hours at each site to explore and to get your pictures. Although this may initially seem daunting, it will give you plenty of time as the pace of life in a penguin colony is very sedate indeed. Take a few minutes at the start to acclimatise and see where the main activity is happening; a good starting point is the landing beach where the penguins leave from and return to after hunting. After that, try the colony, but don't rush around – just sit and absorb it all. The pictures will soon come to you, along with some very friendly penguins!

King penguin, Falkland Islands

Penguins, and especially king penguins, have wonderful shapes for abstracts or close-ups. They are best photographed in late evening light, when they are relaxed after a hard day at sea and the soft light picks out the beautiful detail in their feathers and flippers.

◀ DSLR, 300mm lens with 1.4x teleconverter, 1/125 f8, ISO 100 RAW

Rockhopper penguins, Falkland Islands

Penguins prefer safety in numbers and will hunt at sea in family groups. This gives a great opportunity for a group shot when they return to shore. I hid behind a rock waiting for this group to come ashore so as to avoid disturbing their long walk to the colony.

◀ DSLR, 300mm lens, 1/125 f5.6, ISO 100 RAW, flash

Gentoo penguin, Falkland Islands

Penguins are difficult to expose, especially when wet, so you will have to use one of the exposure shortcuts outlined on p57. Trusting the meter is a recipe for a lot of severely underexposed images, although DSLR users can easily recover these using a RAW converter such as RawShooter premium.

◀ DSLR, 300mm lens, 1/1000 f4, ISO 100 RAW

Gentoo penguin family, Falkland Islands

A hot spot for photography is the colony, which is alive with noise and the sight of chicks dashing after adults and begging for food. Try to pick a low angle and use a long-range zoom to isolate your subject from all the background clutter. Keep your distance, too; 5m from penguins is the recommendation and is close enough to avoid disturbing a vital feeding session.

◀ DSLR, 70-200mm lens with 1.4x teleconverter, 1/60 f11, ISO 100 RAW, flash

REPTILES & AMPHIBIANS

While you may not go out of your way to photograph reptiles and amphibians, there are locations where they are the most visible species. Chameleons, for example, inhabit many regions of the earth and will add a splash of colour to anyone's photography. Snakes need to be treated with extreme caution and should only be approached under the guidance of an expert. Crocodiles and alligators are good for some fun; just remember not to get close enough to become dinner. With larger reptiles such as crocodiles you have a much wider range of photographic options. If you are on a boat, try to go out in the heat of the day as the crocodiles will be out of the water sunning themselves. As a bonus, they open their mouths wide to lose heat, which is great for photographers; it's important to select your autofocus point carefully and focus on the tip of the mouth.

Leaf-tailed gecko, Mantady National Park, Madagascar

Some reptiles have developed amazing camouflage systems so they can avoid becoming someone else's dinner. It took me several minutes to see this leaf-tailed gecko, so complete was its camouflage. Don't be tempted to use flash to brighten this kind of image: the point of the picture is to show how much it blends in with the surroundings, not to make it stand out!

◀ 645 SLR, 90mm macro lens, 1/60 f11, Velvia 50, tripod

Tomato frog, Mantady National Park, Madagascar

Some amphibians rely on having a disgusting taste for their survival, and this tomato frog probably tastes like a boiled old sock (or worse). It can cause severe allergy-like symptoms if eaten and secretes a toxin from its skin so it's best left alone. I used a flash with a diffuser cup to put some soft light onto its back and give a highlight to the eyes.

◀ 645 SLR, 90mm macro lens, 1/125 f8, Velvia 50, flash

Common iguana, Honduras

For this low-angled shot I used an eye-level finder and an aperture of 5.6 to isolate the iguana from its surroundings.

▲ 35mm SLR, 70-200mm lens, 1/125 f5.6, Velvia 50, flash

GROUPS

Most mammals and birds prefer to live in the safety of a herd or flock, as it is a good tactic to have lots of eyes looking out for predators. Whatever their reasons for sticking together, groups of animals and birds make spectacular opportunities for photography, though they are not quite as easy as they seem. Watch out for the overall impression of the group, the colour they generate and the wider view (the habitat), as well as interactions between individuals and patterns.

Flamingos, Lake Nakuru National Park, Kenya

Flamingos are perhaps the most famous coloured birds of all and flocks of them form seas of pink. For this shot I used a zoom lens at the upper end of its range to compress the group and give the impression of great numbers. It's always tempting to use an 81A filter to increase the pink colour, but this nearly always looks false and makes them look more like Martian flamingos!

▲ DSLR, 70-200mm lens, 1/250 f11, ISO 100 RAW

Whooper swans, Hokkaido, Japan

I composed this image of swans to lead deliberately from the front of the frame to the back. I kept the focus squarely on the closest swan and used an aperture of f11 to get as much of the other swans in focus as I could without making the shutter speed too low to hand-hold.

◀ 35mm SLR, 70-200mm lens with 1.4x teleconverter, 1/125 f11, Velvia 50

Ring-tailed lemurs basking in the sun, Réserve Privée de Berenty (Berenty Reserve), Madagascar

With groups it's sometimes best to shoot from a slightly higher angle to isolate individuals. These lemurs were sunbathing in a small clearing so I focused on the one at the front of the image and stood slowly to show each individual in the frame. The stunning red evening light combines with the red sand to add some extra mood.

▲ 645 SLR, 45-85mm lens, 1/60 f16, Velvia 50

Gentoo penguins, Falkland Islands

Sometimes the sheer numbers in a group can make the image confusing, so it pays to look around carefully for the best angle or wait for them to spread out slightly. Also try to show the group in the context of its habitat.

▲ DSLR, 70-200mm lens, 1/400 f8, ISO 50 RAW

NOCTURNAL ANIMALS

It's true to say that most action in the animal kingdom occurs at night. Some species, of course, simply carry on their activity from the pre-dusk hours but an entire night shift of animals also appears and starts to go about their business. In desert regions the change is amazing; sand dunes that are baked to a crisp during the day come alive at night with all manner of critters.

Animals that are exclusively nocturnal require some special care when you are photographing them. The main concern is not to affect their eyesight, which is perfectly attuned to working in the dark but will be blinded for some time if exposed to a direct flash. Unlike their daylight cousins, these animals are not used to human contact and could well be terrified by your presence, so always watch them carefully; if you see any signs of stress, beat a hasty retreat. Here are some simple tips for making the most of your nocturnal opportunities:

▸ **Red eye** Avoid taking a shot when the animal is looking directly at you, or you will get red eye. Mounting the flash on an angled bracket away from the hot shoe reduces this, although it can be a little fiddly on a crowded vehicle.

▸ **Respect** If a predator is hunting it is best to refrain from taking any pictures at all, as you may well reveal its presence and ruin the chance of a successful kill.

▸ **Light quality** Use a flash diffuser cup over the flash to soften the output. This stops the animal from visibly wincing when it fires and also produces a really nice soft light.

▸ **Exposure** Forget trying to work it all out yourself – simply switch the camera to program mode (P) and the flash to TTL (Through the Lens metering) and let them work it out by themselves. If you notice that the exposure is too bright, try applying some minus compensation to the flash.

Grey mouse lemur, Réserve Privée de Berenty, Madagascar
One method of reducing the flash power is to use a torch to light up your subject first. My guide found this grey mouse lemur by torch anyway; he just shone it slightly to one side (not directly into the eyes) and I took a couple of flash pictures before leaving it alone.

▲ 35mm SLR, 70-200mm lens, 1/60 f5.6, Velvia 50, flash

Black rhinoceros, Namib Desert, Namibia

Some water holes in Africa are floodlit, which means that you have no need to use your flash provided you set an ISO of 400.

◀ DSLR, 500mm lens, 1/60 f4, ISO 400 RAW, tripod

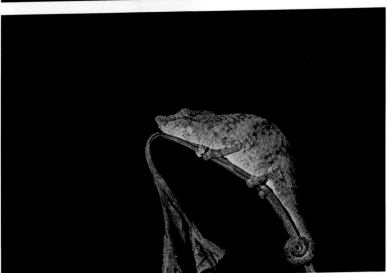

Nose-horned chameleon, Mantady National Park, Madagascar

Unless you are working in the depths of a forest, black backgrounds at night are the norm. This generally keeps the picture free from distracting clutter and focuses the eye on beautiful creatures like this chameleon.

▲ 35mm SLR, 70-200mm lens, 1/60 f5.6, Velvia 50, flash

MARINE LIFE

Most of us are confirmed landlubbers but occasionally the opportunity presents itself to photograph underwater. It doesn't matter if you are photographing tropical fish or great white sharks – the experience of being underwater is fantastic and should not be missed.

Bottle-nosed dolphin, Caribbean

This is almost a night shot. The dolphins were enjoying themselves so much that this one couldn't resist one more jump and, as luck would have it, I had my camera at the ready. You never quite know what animals are likely to do, so always make sure that you're ready to shoot at a moment's notice.

◀ 35mm SLR, 28-70mm F4L lens, 1/800 f4, Provia 100F pushed to 200

Bottlenose dolphin, Honduras

Dolphins are brilliant fun underwater. I only wish I had been using a DSLR at the time because I kept having to return to the boat to change the film.

▲ 35mm underwater SLR, 14mm lens, 1/250 f8, Ektachrome 200

Humpback whale, Silver Banks, Caribbean

I cannot describe the amazing experience of being underwater with whales – I have never experienced anything like it. You forget about everything and just feel incredibly relaxed, which (for me at least) makes a nice change.

◀ 35mm underwater SLR, 14mm, 1/250 f8, Ektachrome 200

Bottle-nosed dolphin, Caribbean

Timing is crucial to action images and this occasion was no exception. When the dolphin would jump was anybody's guess but in time you can get to know the likely pattern of behaviour of an animal. Controlling yourself and your trigger finger is another matter. By waiting till the animal is exactly where you want it in the frame, you can ensure that you don't miss the shot.

◀ 35mm SLR, 17-35mm F4L lens, 1/1000 f5.6, Provia 100F

ELEPHANTS & RHINOS

Elephants and rhinos are particularly well-loved mammals and some of the most impressive on the African savanna. Their huge size and imposing presence makes them extremely attractive to photograph as well as to spend time with. Photographing them is perhaps somewhat limiting as they are potentially dangerous animals, and it is essential that they be treated with the utmost respect. Make sure that your guide also knows these animals well as they can be easy to upset; all it takes is a revving engine or loud chatter. Remain quiet and calm when in close proximity to elephants and rhinos, and ensure that when you stop you do not block their traditional paths (which will be clearly evident on the ground). You should always give way to an elephant or rhino; allow them to pass you and your vehicle in their own time and never attempt to hurry them out of the way, no matter what the urgency.

Elephants have a complex social hierarchy, so watch out for interactions between individuals and especially between mothers and their young. The elephant's trunk and ears and the rhino's horns are the main features of these animals so it pays to make these the important features in your images. Far from being dull and grey and apparently neutral toned, these animals have an uncanny knack of fooling your light meter completely. Their grey skin absorbs light in a way that confuses the light meter, causing overexposure in many cases. It might help to employ the f16 rule or to experiment with other exposure methods described on p57.

White rhinoceros, private game reserve, South Africa

Some African animals look grey and you would expect the light meter to have an easy time of it, but unfortunately it won't. Although rhinos and elephants are grey, their skin absorbs large amounts of light and can cause severe overexposure if the exposure is not corrected. The methods to achieve this are outlined on p57. For this exposure I used the neutral-point method on a nearby log. Remember that the element you use for the metering does not have to be in the shot at all – it just has to be in the same light.

◀ 645 SLR, 45-85mm lens, 1/125 f11, Velvia 50

African elephant swimming in river, Chobe National Park, Botswana

In this chance encounter I had while canoeing across the Chobe River, the elephant was using his trunk as a snorkel. I had no choice but to hand-hold my lens and shoot whatever I could. Luckily, I had my camera ready to shoot any eventuality and thus captured this one-of-a-kind encounter.

▲ 35mm SLR, 100-400mm lens, 1/200 f5.6, ISO 100

African elephant, private game reserve, South Africa

You might think that elephants are always grey and therefore easy to expose on, but you would be mistaken. Elephants come in all sizes, shapes and colours depending on local conditions and lighting – this bronze elephant was captured in the incredible early morning light as it appeared over a nearby mountain range.

◀ 35mm DSLR, 300mm lens, 1/500 f6.3, ISO 100 RAW

FURTHER READING

Cornish, Joe
Scotland's Coast: A Photographer's Journey
Aurum Press, 2005

Estes, Richard D
The Safari Companion: A Guide to Watching African Mammals Including Hoofed Mammals, Carnivores, and Primates
Tutorial Press, 1993

I'Anson, Richard
Travel Photography
Lonely Planet Publications, 2004

Lopez, Barry
Arctic Dreams: Imagination and Desire in a Northern Landscape
Bantam Books, 1986

Munier, Vincent
Tancho
Castor & Pollux, 2004

Prior, Colin
Highland Wilderness
Constable and Robinson, 2004

Rouse, Andy
DSLR Handbook
GMC Publications, 2004

Rouse, Andy
Life in the Wild: A Photographer's Year
GMC Publications, 2002

Rouse, Andy
Wildlife Monographs: Cheetahs
Evans Mitchell Publishers, 2004

Rouse, Andy
Wildlife Monographs: Elephants
Evans Mitchell Publishers, 2004

Rouse, Andy
Wildlife Monographs: Polar Bears
Evans Mitchell Publishers, 2006

Various authors
Light on the Earth
BBC Books, 2005

Webster, Mark
The Art & Technique of Underwater Photography
Voyageur Press, 1998

Wolfe, Art
Rhythms from the Wild
Watson/Guptill-Amphoto Art, 1997

USEFUL WEBSITES

Andy Rouse Wildlife Photography Ltd
www.andyrouse.co.uk

Pixmantec (for RawShooter software)
www.pixmantec.com

Phil Askey's DPReview
www.dpreview.com

Lonely Planet
www.lonelyplanet.com

**Nature Photographers
(online community)**
www.naturephotographers.net

Páramo Outdoor Clothing
www.paramo.co.uk

**Warehouse Express
(for all camera gear)**
www.warehouseexpress.com

INDEX

bold refers to image captions